JUMP START
NODE.JS

BY **DON NGUYEN**

D1065670

Jump Start Node.js

by Don Nguyen

Copyright © 2012 SitePoint Pty. Ltd.

Product Manager: Simon Mackie   **Indexer**: Fred Brown

Technical Editor: Diana MacDonald   **Editor**: Kelly Steele

Expert Reviewer: Giovanni Ferron   **Cover Designer**: Alex Walker

Published by SitePoint Pty. Ltd.

48 Cambridge Street Collingwood
VIC Australia 3066
Web: www.sitepoint.com
Email: business@sitepoint.com

ISBN 978-0-9873321-0-3 (print)

ISBN 978-0-9873321-1-0 (ebook)
Printed and bound in the United States of America

About the Author

Don began his programming career with strongly typed, object-oriented languages such as Java and C++. He used his engineering training to build real-time trading systems designed to be scalable and fault tolerant.

While his first introduction to functional programming was somewhat of a shock to the system, the beauty and elegance of weakly typed dynamic languages such as Python and Ruby shone through. Don has programmed in a variety of web environments including ASP, PHP, and Python, but feels that Node.js is foremost at handling the modern demands of the real-time web.

About the Expert Reviewer

Giovanni Ferron is a web developer currently living in Melbourne, Australia. He has worked for major media companies such as MTV and DMG Radio Australia, and co-founded the website Stereomood.com.[1] A couple of years ago, he fell in love with Node.js and has been spending his nights programming in JavaScript ever since.

About SitePoint

SitePoint specializes in publishing fun, practical, and easy-to-understand content for web professionals. Visit http://www.sitepoint.com/ to access our blogs, books, newsletters, articles, and community forums.

---

[1] http://stereomood.com

This book is dedicated to my Mum and Dad.

To my Dad for his endless patience in driving me to rowing, martial arts, and tennis practice, and for his never-ending support.

To my Mum for cooking dinner with one hand and sketching out the basics of object-oriented programming and database normalization with the other.

Table of Contents

Preface

One of the difficulties I had when trying to learn Node.js was how to get started. The references that I found either dealt with quasi-academic topics such as datagrams and event emitters, or else myopically focused on a topic without regard for the big picture. This book takes you through the complete process of building an application in Node.js. It starts with the canonical "Hello World" example, and goes on to build a real-time web application capable of sending trading information to thousands of connected clients.

What make Node.js different? First, it provides a unified language between the back end and front end. This means that all your thinking can be in a single language, with no cognitive overhead when switching from front end to back. Furthermore, it allows for shared code libraries and templates. This opens up a lot of interesting possibilities, the surface of which is just beginning to be properly explored.

Second, it's fast. One of the common complaints of interpreted languages such as PHP, Python, and Ruby is speed. Jason Hoffman, CTO of Joyent, has discussed how Node.js is at the point where its performance can break operating systems. A single core with less than 1GB of RAM is capable of handling 10GB of traffic and one million connected end points. Combining 24 of these into a single machine produces an overall level of throughput that exceeds the capacity of operating systems and TCP/IP stacks. In other words, with a properly designed application it's not Node.js that's the bottleneck—it's your operating system.

Third, its nonblocking architecture is made for the real-time web. JavaScript was chosen as a language because it's based on nonblocking callbacks and has a very small core API. This means it was possible to build the entire Node.js ecosystem around nonblocking packages, of which there are currently in excess of ten thousand. The end result is a platform and ecosystem that architecturally fits perfectly with the modern demands of the real-time web.

I trust by now that you're excited by the possibilities of what Node.js can do for your real-time application. By the end of this book, I'm confident that you'll have the skills to be able to start dissecting and solving all but the most esoteric of problems. There is no greater joy in software than solving a complicated task and thinking at the end of it, "That was all I had to do!" It is one I've experienced many times working with Node.js, and it's my hope that you enjoy the same satisfaction both throughout the book and in using Node.js to solve your real-world problems.

Who Should Read This Book

This book is aimed at two target audiences. You might be a front-end engineer who is interested in looking at server-side development. An existing knowledge of JavaScript will prove useful, even if you are unfamiliar with certain server-side engineering techniques. Rest assured that by the end of the book, the topic will be covered in sufficient detail for you to know how to apply your front-end skills to back-end problems.

The second potential reader is the server-side engineer who uses another language such as PHP, Python, Ruby, Java, or .NET. The main benefit you'll derive is seeing how your existing architectural, design, and pattern knowledge is applied to the world of Node.js. You may have little to no knowledge of JavaScript, but this should pose no big hindrance. By design, it's an easy language to learn, and we will have covered many examples of both its syntax and idiosyncratic features by the end of the book.

What's in This Book

This book comprises the following seven chapters.

Chapter 1: *Coming to a Server Near You*
Node.js is introduced and its features and benefits explained. We then build a simple application to introduce Node.js. The application sends data from a form to MongoDB, a NoSQL database.

Chapter 2: *Let's Get Functional*
This chapter introduces programming with Node.js in a functional style. We'll build a stock exchange trading engine that's capable of accepting orders and matching trades.

Chapter 3: *Persistence Pays*
Here we explore MongoDB. I'll explain the use cases of MongoDB and how it compares to traditional SQL databases. We'll then look at the MongoDB query language and show how it can be integrated with your Node.js projects.

Chapter 4: *Beautifying with Bootstrap*

Bootstrap is a front-end framework from Twitter that makes it easy to build professional-looking sites. We'll look at some of the most common widgets and use them to build a login screen and stock portfolio tracker.

Chapter 5: *The Real-time Web*

In this chapter we examine Socket.IO. We'll see how learning one simple API can allow real-time communication across a range of projects without needing to worry about browser versions or communications protocols.

Chapter 6: *Backbone*

We'll discuss how frameworks are useful in managing client-side JavaScript in this chapter. We'll then show how Backbone.js can be incorporated into your project by updating trades in the browser in real time.

Chapter 7: *Production*

In the final chapter, we'll look at the main differences between a development and production environment. We'll cover various deployment options before getting our application deployed and running live!

Where to Find Help

Node.js represents a paradigm shift in web development, providing a unifying language all the way from the front end to the back end. It has experienced a boom in popularity on GitHub, so chances are good that by the time you read this, some minor detail or other of the Node.js platform will have changed from what's described in this book. Thankfully, SitePoint has a thriving community of JavaScript developers ready and waiting to help you out if you run into trouble, and we also maintain a list of known errata for this book that you can consult for the latest updates.

The SitePoint Forums

The SitePoint Forums[1] are discussion forums where you can ask questions about anything related to web development. You may, of course, answer questions, too. That's how a discussion forum site works—some people ask, some people answer and most people do a bit of both. Sharing your knowledge benefits others and strengthens the community. A lot of fun and experienced web designers and de-

---

[1] http://www.sitepoint.com/forums/

velopers hang out there. It's a good way to learn new stuff, have questions answered in a hurry, and just have fun.

The JavaScript & jQuery Forum[2] is probably the best place to head to ask any questions.

The Book's Website

Located at http://www.sitepoint.com/books/nodejs1/, the website that supports this book will give you access to the following facilities:

The Code Archive

As you progress through this book, you'll note a number of references to the code archive. This is a downloadable ZIP archive that contains each and every line of example source code that's printed in this book. If you want to cheat (or save yourself from carpal tunnel syndrome), go ahead and download the archive.[3]

Updates and Errata

No book is perfect, and we expect that watchful readers will be able to spot at least one or two mistakes before the end of this one. The Errata page on the book's website will always have the latest information about known typographical and code errors.

The SitePoint Newsletters

In addition to books like this one, SitePoint publishes free email newsletters such as the *SitePoint* newsletter, *JSPro*, *PHPMaster*, *CloudSpring*, *RubySource*, *Design-Festival*, and *BuildMobile*. In them you'll read about the latest news, product releases, trends, tips, and techniques for all aspects of web development. Sign up to one or more of these newsletters at http://www.sitepoint.com/newsletter/.

Your Feedback

If you're unable to find an answer through the forums, or if you wish to contact SitePoint for any other reason, the best place to write is books@sitepoint.com. We have a well-staffed email support system set up to track your inquiries, and if our

---

[2] http://www.sitepoint.com/forums/forumdisplay.php?15-JavaScript-amp-jQuery
[3] http://www.sitepoint.com/books/nodejs1/code.php

support team members are unable to answer your question, they'll send it straight to us. Suggestions for improvements, as well as notices of any mistakes you may find, are especially welcome.

Friends of SitePoint

Thanks for buying this book. We really appreciate your support! We now think of you as a "Friend of SitePoint," and so would like to invite you to our special "Friends of SitePoint" page.[4] Here you can SAVE up to 43% on a range of other super-cool SitePoint products, just by using the password: **friends**.

Online Quiz

Once you've mastered Node.js, test yourself with our online quiz. With questions based on the book's content, only true Node.js ninjas can achieve a perfect score. Head on over to http://quizpoint.com/#categories/NODE.JS.

Acknowledgments

I'd like to thank the wonderful team at SitePoint for guiding me through the process of publishing my first book: to Simon Mackie for patiently answering all my questions and keeping everything on track; to Giovanni Ferron for reviewing my code and pointing out bugs; to Diana MacDonald for ensuring clarity in my code; to Kelly Steele for keeping my English stylistically and grammatically correct; and to Alex Walker for the wonderful cover art.

To my longtime friends, Jarrod Mirabito and Andrew Prolov: thanks for helping review my initial work long before it was even a book proposal. To my flatmate, Angelo Aspris: thanks for patiently accepting "busy writing" as an excuse for long stretches of absenteeism. To Andy Walker: thanks for keeping the flame of entrepreneurship burning brightly. To my lifelong friend Chuong Mai-Viet: thanks for dragging me away from the desk on bright and sunny days to keep my golf handicap down and my Vitamin D intake up.

---

[4] http://sitepoint.com/friends

Conventions Used in This Book

You'll notice that we've used certain typographic and layout styles throughout this book to signify different types of information. Look out for the following items.

Code Samples

Code in this book will be displayed using a fixed-width font, like so:

```
<h1>A Perfect Summer's Day</h1>
<p>It was a lovely day for a walk in the park. The birds
were singing and the kids were all back at school.</p>
```

If the code is to be found in the book's code archive, the name of the file will appear at the top of the program listing, like this:

```
example.css
.footer {
  background-color: #CCC;
  border-top: 1px solid #333;
}
```

If only part of the file is displayed, this is indicated by the word *excerpt*:

```
example.css (excerpt)
  border-top: 1px solid #333;
```

If additional code is to be inserted into an existing example, the new code will be displayed in bold:

```
function animate() {
  new_variable = "Hello";
}
```

Also, where existing code is required for context, rather than repeat all the code, a ⋮ will be displayed:

```
function animate() {
  ⋮
  return new_variable;
}
```

Some lines of code are intended to be entered on one line, but we've had to wrap them because of page constraints. A ➡ indicates a line break that exists for formatting purposes only, and should be ignored.

```
URL.open("http://jspro.com/raw-javascript/how-to-create-custom-even
➡ts-in-javascript/");
```

Tips, Notes, and Warnings

Hey, You!

Tips will give you helpful little pointers.

Ahem, Excuse Me ...

Notes are useful asides that are related—but not critical—to the topic at hand. Think of them as extra tidbits of information.

Make Sure You Always ...

... pay attention to these important points.

Watch Out!

Warnings will highlight any gotchas that are likely to trip you up along the way.

Coming to a Server Near You

"You see things and you say, 'Why?' But I dream things that never were, and I say, 'Why not?'"

—George Bernard Shaw

Why Node.js?

If a picture speaks a thousand words, what would it take to speak a thousand pictures? Or for that matter, an infinite number of pictures? My first introduction to Node.js was through WordSquared,[1] seen in Figure 1.1. This is an online, real-time, infinite game of Scrabble built using the same technologies that we'll discuss in this book. As soon as I set eyes on the game, I had to find out more about the technology behind it, and I hope you feel the same.

What's incredible about the game is that it was prototyped in just 48 hours as part of Node.js Knockout.[2] Bryan Cantrill, VP of Engineering at Joyent (which manufactures Node.js) has said that when doing things in Node.js, you sometimes get the feeling of "Is this it? Surely it needs to be more complicated." This is a sentiment

---

[1] http://wordsquared.com/
[2] http://nodeknockout.com/

I share. Node.js is a joy to work with, and I intend to share that with you through the code we'll write throughout this book.

Figure 1.1. WordSquared: a way to examine Node.js in action

Node.js is a server-side JavaScript platform that consists of a deliberately minimalist core library alongside a rich ecosystem. It runs atop the V8 JavaScript engine, which makes it very fast thanks to the talented engineers at Google. JavaScript is popular on the client side, but it was chosen as the target language primarily for engineering considerations, the details of which will be discussed as the chapter unfolds.

The home page of Node.js describes it thus:

> "Node.js is a platform built on Chrome's JavaScript runtime for easily building fast, scalable network applications. Node.js uses an event-driven, non-blocking I/O model that makes it lightweight and efficient, perfect for data-intensive real-time applications that run across distributed devices."
>
> —http://nodejs.org/

This may seem cryptic to newcomers, but it succinctly summarizes some of the key strengths of Node.js and is worth exploring in more detail. People are often taken aback when they hear that JavaScript is the targeted programming language. That's because there's a perception in the programming community that JavaScript is not a "real" language such as C, C++, or Java. Yet JavaScript did have its genesis as an interpreted language for the browser; the "Java" part of the name was actually chosen to capitalize upon the perceived popularity of the Java programming language at the time.

Since its humble beginnings, JavaScript has proliferated and is now supported in every major web browser, including those on mobile devices. Not only is it a popular language, but the tools and frameworks currently available for it make it qualify as a powerful engineering tool. JavaScript as a server-side platform supports continuous integration, continuous deployment, connections to relational databases, service-oriented architecture, and just about every other technique available to its more well-established brethren.

In conjunction with Google's V8 JavaScript engine, it is now extremely fast; in fact, it's several times faster than other scripted languages such as Ruby and Python. Against Python3, JavaScript V8 Engine has a median benchmark 13 times as fast with a roughly similar code size.[3] Against Ruby 1.9, the median benchmark is eight times as fast.[4] These are incredible benchmarks for a dynamic language, and are due in no small part to V8 optimizations such as compilation into machine code pre-execution.

 On Benchmarking

Benchmarking is an intricate topic,[5] and the numbers above should be taken with the proverbial grain of salt. Whenever any discussion of benchmarking arises, it is generally qualified with "it depends." The main purpose of discussing the benchmark was to dispel any misconception of JavaScript being inherently slow.

The official description talks about the event-driven, non-blocking I/O model. Traditionally, programming is done in a synchronous manner: a line of code is executed, the system waits for the result, the result is processed, and then execution resumes. Sometimes waiting for the result can take a long time; for example, reading from a database or writing to a network.

In languages such as Java and C#, one solution is to spawn a new **thread**. A thread may be thought of as a lightweight process that performs tasks. Threaded programming can be difficult because multiple threads can be trying to access the same resource concurrently. Without dissecting the intricacies of multi-threaded programming, you can imagine it would be disastrous for one thread to be incrementing a counter while another thread is decrementing the counter at the same time.

---

[3] http://shootout.alioth.debian.org/u32/benchmark.php? test=all&lang=v8&lang2=python3

[4] http://shootout.alioth.debian.org/u32/benchmark.php? test=all&lang=v8&lang2=yarv

[5] http://shootout.alioth.debian.org/dont-jump-to-conclusions.php

JavaScript approaches the problem differently. There is only ever a single thread. When doing slow I/O operations such as reading a database, the program does not wait. Instead, it immediately continues to the next line of code. When the I/O operation returns, it triggers a callback function and the result can be processed. If the mechanics of this seems slightly counterintuitive, rest assured that by the end of the book it will be second nature, because we'll be seeing this pattern over and over again. Node.js offers a simple, fast, event-driven programming model well-suited to the asynchronous nature of modern-day web applications.

Strengths and Weaknesses

Node.js is not a panacea. There is a certain class of problems in which its strengths shine through. Computer programs can be generally classified according to whether they are CPU bound or I/O bound. **CPU bound** problems benefit from an increase in the number of clock cycles available for computation. Prime number calculation is a good example. Node.js, however, is not designed to deal with these CPU bound problems. Even before Node.js formally existed, Ryan Dahl proposed the following:[6]

> "There is a strict requirement that any request calculates for at most, say, 5ms before returning to the event loop. If you break the 5ms limit, then your request handler is never run again (request handlers will be tied to a certain path/method, I think). If your uploaded server-side JavaScript is stupid and is blocking (… it calculates the first 10,000 primes) then it will be killed before completion.
>
> …
>
> Web developers need this sort of environment where it is not possible for them to do stupid things. Ruby, Python, C++, [and] PHP are all terrible languages for web development because they allow too much freedom."
>
> —Ryan Dahl

I/O bound problems are alleviated by increased throughput in I/O such as disk, memory, and network bandwidth, and improved data caching. Many problems are I/O bound, and it's in this domain that Node.js truly shines. Take, for example, the

---

[6] http://four.livejournal.com/963421.html

C10K problem,[7] which poses the dilemma of how to handle ten thousand or more concurrent connections for a web server. Some technology platforms are ill-equipped for managing this type of capacity and require various patches and workarounds. Node.js excels at this task because it's based on a nonblocking, asynchronous architecture designed for concurrency.

I hope I've whetted your appetite; it is now time to begin.

 On Speed

> The book's core project involves building a real-time stock market trading engine that will stream live prices into a web browser. The more inquisitive among you may ask, "Shouldn't a stock market trading engine be built using a language such as C for faster-than-light, jaw-dropping speed?" If we were building a stock market engine for actual trading, my answer would be "Yes."
>
> The main goal of this book is to transfer the skill set rather than the actual project into the real world. There is a narrow domain of "hard" real-time applications such as a stock exchange where specialized software and hardware are required because microseconds count. However, there is a much larger number of "soft" real-time applications such as Facebook, Twitter, and eBay where microseconds are of small consequence. This is Node.js's speciality, and you'll understand how to build these types of applications by the end of this book.

In the Beginning

Let's run through installing Node.js, setting up a web framework, building a basic form page, and connecting to a database.

Installation

It is possible to install Node.js from the raw source code, but it's much simpler to install using a package manager.

Go to https://github.com/joyent/node/wiki/Installing-Node.js-via-package-manager and follow the instructions for your particular distribution. There are currently instructions for Gentoo, Debian, Ubuntu, openSUSE and SLE (SUSE Linux Enterprises),

---

[7] http://en.wikipedia.org/wiki/C10k_problem

Fedora, and RHEL/CentOS, as well as several other Linux distributions. Windows and Mac OS X instructions are also available.

After installation, type node at the command line to bring up the read-eval-print loop (REPL). You can test your installation by typing:

```
console.log('Hello world')
```

You should receive:

```
Hello world

undefined
```

If you did, congratulations! You have just written your first Node.js program. The console always prints out the return type. This is why Hello world is followed by undefined. Now that you've written the canonical Hello world program, I'm happy to inform you that it will be the first and last boring program you'll see in this book. To prove my point, we'll now jump straight in and build an authentication module to verify usernames and passwords using cloud-based NoSQL technology. (If you're scratching your head and wondering what this means, don't worry—all will be revealed shortly!)

So what is **cloud-based NoSQL** technology, and why should you care? There's been a lot of hype around cloud-based technology. For our purposes, cloud technology is useful because it allows our applications to scale: additional virtual servers can be brought online with just a few mouse clicks.

The NoSQL movement is relatively recent and, as such, it is difficult to arrive at a comprehensive definition of what the technology encompasses. Broadly, it can be thought of as a family of database technologies built for handling large masses of unstructured and semi-structured data. Companies such as Google, Amazon, and Facebook make extensive use of NoSQL technology to house the vast quantities of data generated by their users.

For this book, we will be using MongoDB as our NoSQL database for reasons that will be fleshed out in more detail in Chapter 3. MongoDB is a mature and scalable document-oriented database that has been deployed successfully in enterprise environments such as foursquare and craigslist.[8] A **document-oriented database** is a database where the traditional database row is replaced with a less structured document, such as XML or JSON. MongoDB allows ad hoc queries and so retains much of the flexibility that SQL offers. I've chosen MongoLab[9] as a cloud provider for our stock monitoring application because it has a generous free hosting plan in place.

Assembling the Pieces

The first step is to go to MongoLab, seen in Figure 1.2, and sign up an account. Then click on **Create New** next to Databases. Leave the cloud provider as Amazon EC2 and select the free pricing plan. Choose a database name, a username, and password.

Now we'll set up the web framework. Node.js provides a built-in, bare-bones HTTP server. Built on top of this is Connect, a middleware framework that provides support for cookies, sessions, logging, and compression, to name a few.[10] On top of Connect is Express, which has support for routing, templates (using the Jade templating engine), and view rendering.[11] Throughout this book we'll predominantly use Express.

Figure 1.2. Signing up to MongoLab

Express can be installed with the following command:

```
sudo npm install -g express@2.5.8
```

---

[8] http://api.mongodb.org/wiki/current/Production%20Deployments.html
[9] http://mongolab.com
[10] http://www.senchalabs.org/connect/
[11] http://expressjs.com/guide.html

We use the -g switch to indicate that the package should be installed globally and @2.5.8 to indicate the version we'll use in this book.

 Global versus Local

On the official Node.js blog, sparing use of global installs is recommended.[12] The guideline is to use a global install if the package needs to be accessed on the command line, and a local install if it needs to be accessed in your program. In some cases—such as Express where both are required—it's fine to do both.

An application with basic default options can be created using this command:

```
express authentication
```

You should see output similar to the following:

```
create : authentication
create : authentication/package.json
⋮

dont forget to install dependencies:
$ cd authentication && npm install
```

To explain the last line ($ cd authentication && npm install), npm install will install packages according to the dependencies specified in **package.json**. This is a plain-text file that specifies package dependencies in JavaScript Object Notation. For this project, modify **package.json** to contain the following text:

chapter01/authentication/package.json *(excerpt)*

```
{
    "name": "authentication"
  , "version": "0.0.1"
  , "private": true
  , "dependencies": {
      "express": "2.5.8"
    , "jade": "0.26.1"
```

[12] http://blog.nodejs.org/2011/03/23/npm-1-0-global-vs-local-installation/

```
   , "mongoose": "2.6.5"
   }
}
```

 Avoiding Dependency Hell

Instead of a particular version number, it's possible to specify "*", which will retrieve the latest version from the repository. While it may be tempting to always
work with the latest version, just because your application is compatible with one
version, it in no way guarantees that it will still be compatible with the next. I
recommend always stating the version number at the very least. Even this is no
guarantee of correctness. If you use a package that employs the "*" syntax, you
will run into a similar problem. For a more robust solution, I recommend you
look into Shrinkwrap.[13]

These dependencies can then be installed by changing to the **authentication** directory
(cd authentication) and typing npm install. Then type node app, and after
navigating to http://localhost:3000 in your browser, you should see the message,
"Welcome to Express." Easy, wasn't it?

A Basic Form

The next step is to create a basic form to post data to the server. With a web server
such as Apache, you'd normally place a file into a directory to be served to the user.
Node.js is deliberately minimalist, with very little that is automatically done. If you
wish to read a file from the disk, you'll need to explicitly program it. Kill your app
and, at the top of **app.js**, add the fs dependency to allow reading from the file system.
Then add the **/form** route:

chapter01/authentication/app.js *(excerpt)*

```
var express = require('express')
  , routes = require('./routes')
  , fs = require('fs');
  ⋮
// Routes
app.get('/', routes.index);
```

---

[13] http://blog.nodejs.org/2012/02/27/managing-node-js-dependencies-with-shrinkwrap/

```
app.get('/form', function(req, res) { ①
  fs.readFile('./form.html', function(error, content) { ②
    if (error) {
      res.writeHead(500);
      res.end();
    }
    else {
      res.writeHead(200, { 'Content-Type': 'text/html' });
      res.end(content, 'utf-8');
    }
  });
});
```

The above listing has several important features.

① This line handles all the routing to **/form**. Whenever anybody makes a request to http://localhost:3000/form, Express captures the request and it is handled by the code within.

② This line attempts to read **form.html** from the file system and serve the HTML file. If there's an error, a 500 response will be sent back to the browser.

Callback Functions

This is the first time we've broached callback functions, which might be tricky for those starting from other languages. As an example, type the following into a file named **cb.js**:

```
setTimeout(function() {console.log('first or second');}
  , 500);
console.log('we will see');
```

Run `node cb` and note the text order. The first line sets a timeout for a function to be executed in 500ms. The program immediately resumes execution, which is why `we will see` is printed before `first or second`.

In Node.js, everything is asynchronous by design, so only your own code will block a process. The first line in this code sample could be any I/O operation including reading and writing from databases and networks. In every instance, nothing I/O-related will block and the rest of your program will immediately execute. This paradigm can be confusing at first, but you'll see it's quite an elegant solution once you start to gain familiarity with it.

We can create a very simple **form.html** as follows:

chapter01/authentication/form.html

```html
<form action="/signup" method="post">
  <div>
    <label>Username:</label>
    <input type="text" name="username"/><br/>
  </div>
  <div>
    <label>Password:</label>
    <input type="password" name="password"/>
  </div>
  <div><input type="submit" value="Sign Up"/></div>
</form>
```

When you visit http://localhost:3000/form, you should see your form rendered in the page as in Figure 1.3.

Figure 1.3. Form screen

Not quite what you imagined Web 2.0 to look like? Never mind, we'll cover styling your page in a subsequent chapter. There's enough to absorb at the moment without concerning yourself with how to make your elements shine on the page.

When a user clicks on the **Sign Up** button, the form data will be posted to **/signup**. We'll now set up a handler in Express to process the form data. Copy the following code into **app.js** where you left off:

chapter01/authentication/app.js *(excerpt)*

```js
app.post('/signup', function(req, res) {
  var username = req.body.username;
  var password = req.body.password;
  User.addUser(username, password, function(err, user) {
```

```
    if (err) throw err;
    res.redirect('/form');
  });
});
```

The first line of this code listing is similar to what we've seen before except that `app.get` is replaced with `app.post`. The next two lines extract the username and password from the request object. The next line `User.addUser(username, password, function(err, user) {` looks a little mysterious. Where does `User` come from? It comes from the users module, which we'll create shortly. Node.js comes with an excellent module system that allows the programmer to encapsulate functions. Separation of concerns is a core programming principle for managing complexity, and Node.js makes it easy to write modules that perform specific, well-defined tasks. After adding the user, we redirect back to the form page.

 Real-world Development

In the real world, Express provides a lot of useful abstractions. This means that in future it won't be necessary to read files from the disk in the manner we are now. Note also that, by default, Node.js does not support "hot swapping" of code, meaning that changes are only reflected when you restart Node.js. This can become tedious after a while, so I suggest at some point you install node-supervisor to automatically restart the system upon changes to the file.[14]

The Database

In order to create a users module, we'll need to write a database module. Place the following code into a file called **db.js** in a directory called **lib**:

chapter01/authentication/lib/db.js

```
var mongoose = require('mongoose');
var Schema = mongoose.Schema;

module.exports.mongoose = mongoose;
module.exports.Schema = Schema;

// Connect to cloud database
```

---

[14] https://github.com/isaacs/node-supervisor

```
var username = "user"
var password = "password";
var address = ' @dbh42.mongolab.com:27427/nockmarket';
connect();

// Connect to mongo
function connect() {
  var url = 'mongodb://' + username + ':' + password + address;
  mongoose.connect(url);
}
function disconnect() {mongoose.disconnect()}
```

It is surprisingly simple to connect to a cloud-based NoSQL provider. You will need to replace `username`, `password`, and `address` with your own personal details. For example, `var username = "user"` might become `var username = "bob927"`. MongoLab provides a user tab for adding new users, seen in Figure 1.4.

Figure 1.4. The **Users** tab in MongoLab

Figure 1.5 shows where you can obtain the database address.

Figure 1.5. Obtaining the address in MongoLab

We will use the Mongoose package, which allows a connection from Node.js to MongoDB. `module.exports` is the Node.js syntax for exposing functions and variables to other modules.

We will expose the Mongoose driver as well as the Mongoose `Schema` object. A **schema** is simply a way to define the structure of a collection. In this case, our schema consists of a `username` string and a `password` string. Other than that, we define functions to connect and disconnect from the database.

The next step is to define the user module. Place this code in a file called **User.js** in a directory called **models**:

```
chapter01/authentication/models/User.js (excerpt)

var db = require('../lib/db');

var UserSchema = new db.Schema({
    username : {type: String, unique: true}
  , password : String
})

var MyUser = db.mongoose.model('User', UserSchema);

// Exports
module.exports.addUser = addUser;

// Add user to database
function addUser(username, password, callback) {
  var instance = new MyUser();
  instance.username = username;
  instance.password = password;
  instance.save(function (err) {
    if (err) {
      callback(err);
    }
    else {
      callback(null, instance);
    }
  });
}
```

We begin by importing our previously defined database module and defining a simple schema. We can then instantiate a new user, set the username and password, and save to the database using the **save** function. If there's an error, we send it to the callback function. Otherwise, we send back the actual user object.

Password Security

In this example, we store the raw password in the database, which presents a security risk. Normally, the password would be encrypted. There are other secure techniques based on salting the encrypted password to make it more resistant to dictionary attack.

We are now ready to integrate our user module with Express. This involves adding one additional line of import code to our **app.js** file:

chapter01/authentication/app.js *(excerpt)*

```
var express = require('express')
  , routes = require('./routes')
  , fs = require('fs')
  , User = require('./models/User.js');
```

Now if you restart your app and submit your form, you should see the data appear in MongoLab, as in Figure 1.6.

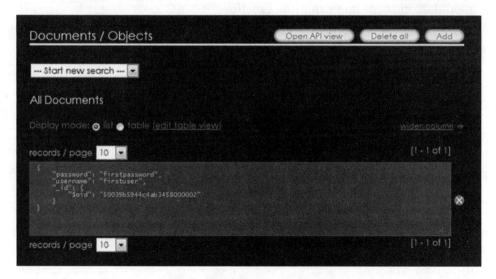

Figure 1.6. New user data in MongoLab

Note that the collection "users" (which can loosely be thought of as a table) was created automatically. That's all there is to building your very first cloud-enabled NoSQL solution. If your next project begins to take on the popularity of Facebook or Twitter, your infrastructure will be ready to scale!

Directory Structures

It might seem a little convoluted to be storing a single file in a separate directory, but as your code base grows larger, it is necessary to group files together in a logical manner to enhance understandability and maintainability. By convention, I put database models into a **models** directory, and business logic and supporting functions into a **lib** directory.

Summary

In this chapter, we've covered the following:

- the philosophy behind Node.js and what makes it different from other programming environments
- installing Node.js
- executing programs from the console using the read-eval-print loop
- building a basic Express application
- basic package management
- modularizing code and exporting functions
- submitting data to a form
- storing data in MongoDB using the cloud platform from MongoLab

Chapter 2

Let's Get Functional

> "I have always wished for my computer to be as easy to use as my telephone; my wish has come true because I can no longer figure out how to use my telephone."
>
> —Bjarne Stroustrup, creator of C++

Introduction

JavaScript is sometimes dismissed as a language used by developers who do a search on the Web, grab a random script, and make a web page to perform a certain task. In this chapter, we are going to dispel that myth once and for all. We'll do this by building a stock exchange trading engine that's perfectly capable of accepting orders and executing trades in a manner similar to NASDAQ or the New York Stock Exchange. We will call our fictional exchange the nockmarket, which is short for the Node.js stock market. Before you protest that your finance or IT knowledge is incapable of absorbing the intricacies of such a task, rest assured that it's simple once you break down the problem into the relevant components.

Let's start with a basic scenario, an empty stock exchange. Suppose you wish to buy some Facebook stock for $40. You submit an order to the exchange to buy 100 units of stock. As there are no sellers at this time, your order sits in the book waiting for a matching offer as portrayed in Figure 2.1.

Figure 2.1. Wishing to buy Facebook stock at $40

Suppose a second person comes along and wishes to sell 200 units of their stock for $41. This is not quite the price you were asking for, and now both orders are sitting in the book as shown in Figure 2.2.

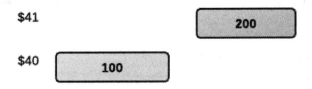

Figure 2.2. An offer for 200 units @ $41 is rejected

At long last, a third person comes along wishing to sell 75 units for $40. The price is right: 75 units will be traded at $40. Figure 2.3 shows what the order book will look like once this transaction is completed: your remaining buy order of 25 units at a price of $40 and the 200 untraded units belonging to person number two at $41.

Trade, 75 @ $40

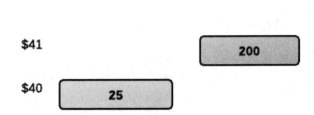

Figure 2.3. After a trade of 75 units @ $40

I trust this example is easy to follow. It comprises all the finance knowledge you'll require to understand our example application.

Always Be Testing

The next piece of the puzzle is transforming the aforementioned scenarios into code. We will do this by following **test-driven development**. This means that we write unit tests first, all of which will fail. We then write the implementation until all the unit tests are working correctly.

Let's start with the simplest possible scenario to flesh out a stock exchange API. First, we wish to buy some stock, which suggests the existence of a buy function. In terms of its parameters, price and volume are obvious components.

Therefore, if we were buying 100 units at a price of $40, our first pass at an API might look like:

```
exchange.buy(40, 100)
```

While this line of code may appear simple, it is actually very close to the final product. What's missing is the concept of **state**. In other words, when processing an order, how do we know about all the orders that have preceded it? There are two primary schools of thought. In **object-oriented programming**, the state is generally stored internally to the exchange object. The exchange object after an order differs to the exchange object before an order due to a state change.

In **functional programming**, functions generally have no side effects. This means that commonly we send inputs and receive outputs in an **immutable** manner. The input remains unchanged and the exchange object is exactly the same before and after an order. Both programming styles are excellent paradigms, with JavaScript supporting both. For this book, I have chosen to write code in a functional style, although object-oriented would also have been a fine choice.

Programming in a functional style requires that we add a third parameter to pass the state of the order book into our function. This means that we modify the aforesaid example as follows:

```
exchange.buy(40, 100, exchangeData)
```

exchangeData is an object that contains the full state of the order book. Our function will process the order and return a new object representing the new state of the order book.

Time to translate this into code. Throughout the book we'll use a testing framework called Mocha.[1] Mocha makes it easy to perform asynchronous unit tests and specifically supports the test-driven paradigm that we've discussed. It can output results in a variety of formats, making it easy to integrate with other testing tools.

Create a new folder to house this chapter's project and within it create a subdirectory called **test**. Within **test**, create a file called **exchange.test.js** and enter the following:

chapter02/test/exchange.test.js *(excerpt)*

```
test('buy should add a BUY nockmarket order', function(done) {
});
```

The first part of any test is to provide a plain English description of what the test does. Therefore, even somebody completely unfamiliar with programming should have an understanding of what the test is trying to accomplish. This way, when unit tests fail it's easy to gain an understanding of what is failing without having to mentally process large blocks of code.

Now we can write the actual test case:

chapter02/test/exchange.test.js *(excerpt)*

```
test('buy should add a BUY nockmarket order', function(done) {
    exchangeData = exchange.buy(40, 100, exchangeData); ❶
    exchangeData.buys.volumes[40].should.eql(100); ❷
    done(); ❸
});
```

❶   First, we submit an order to the exchange using our buy function.

❷   Then we check to see that, on the buy side, at a price of $40 there are exactly 100 units available.

should.eql(100) may look understandable while still mysterious. Understandable in the sense that it's evident what it is checking for, but mysterious because it's not immediately obvious where it comes from. Here, we're using the should.js assertion library,[2] where you'll find a more detailed description on

---

[1] http://visionmedia.github.com/mocha/
[2] https://github.com/visionmedia/should.js/tree/

the home page. I will cherry-pick a few examples and include them here so that you can gain an understanding of the syntax and how it should be used:

```
[].should.be.empty
[1,2,3].should.eql([1,2,3])
user.age.should.be.within(5, 50)
'test'.should.be.a('string')
user.age.should.not.be.above(100)
```

❸ Lastly, done is a callback function indicating to Mocha that we're ready for the next test. Mocha runs **serially**, which means that each unit test is fully completed before moving onto the next test. It's an elegant way of handling the asynchronous nature of JavaScript. So far, we've not worried ourselves with implementation details; we've just written the test. One of the benefits of test-driven design is that it forces you to think more like a software architect. When you write the tests, you imagine the API that clients might need to use and then plan accordingly.

The sell case is analogous to the buy case:

chapter02/test/exchange.test.js *(excerpt)*

```
test('sell should add a SELL nockmarket order', function(done) {
    exchangeData = exchange.sell(41, 200, exchangeData); ❶
    exchangeData.sells.volumes['41'].should.eql(200); ❷
    done();
});
```

❶ First, we use our sell function to submit an order to sell 200 units at $41.

❷ Then we check to see that, on the sell side, there are 200 units available at the price of $41.

Trading does involve some extra details:

chapter02/test/exchange.test.js *(excerpt)*

```
test('sell should produce trades', function(done) {
    exchangeData = exchange.sell(40, 75, exchangeData); ❶
    exchangeData.trades[0].price.should.eql(40); ❷
    exchangeData.trades[0].volume.should.eql(75); ❸
```

```
exchangeData.buys.volumes[40].should.eql(25);  ❹
exchangeData.sells.volumes[41].should.eql(200);  ❺
done();
});
```

❶ First, similar to the previous examples, we submit a sell order for 75 units at $40.

❷ This results in a trade of 75 units at a price of $40, as in Figure 2.3. We store trades in an array; therefore, the first trade should occur at a price of $40 ...

❸ ... And a volume of 75. Now that we have tested the trades, we also need to check the new state of the order book.

❹ After the trade on the buy side, we should have 25 units at a price of $40.

❺ On the sell side, we should have 200 units at a price of $41.

The following code sets up some empty exchange data and imports modules required for testing:

chapter02/test/exchange.test.js *(excerpt)*

```
'use strict';

var assert = require('assert')
  , should = require('should');

var exchangeData = {};

suite('exchange', function() {
 … // place existing test cases here
});
```

If we wrap our test cases in this code, they'll be ready to run.

Strict Mode

JavaScript as a language is extremely permissive. Some people would argue it is too permissive, because it allows a number of programming techniques that fall short of best practice. `use strict` is a feature that will generate errors when some of these lesser programming techniques are used. One example of such techniques is trying to assign a value to a variable where it hasn't been defined. John Resig, creator of jQuery, has written a good summary.[3] I recommend always using strict mode in your own code.

package.json in the root directory should contain the following:

chapter02/package.json *(excerpt)*

```
{
    "name": "nockmarket"
,   "version": "0.0.1"
,   "private": true
,   "dependencies": {
        "jquery" : "1.7.3"
    ,   "mocha": "1.3.0"
    ,   "should": "1.0.0"
    }
}
```

Mocha uses `make` to run the test harness. If you're unfamiliar with `make`, the details aren't important. All you need to do is create a file called **Makefile** (with no file extension) as follows:

chapter02/Makefile

```
test:
    @./node_modules/.bin/mocha -u tdd
.PHONY: test
```

For the second line you must have a tab as the very first character, as spaces will fail to work. This will run the mocha binary. The `tdd` indicates test-driven design.

From here, run `npm install` followed by `make test`. (Note that Mac OS X requires Xcode Command Line Tools to be installed to use the `make` command. Windows users will need to install Cygwin or an equivalent.) The beginning of your output should resemble the following:

[3] http://ejohn.org/blog/ecmascript-5-strict-mode-json-and-more/

```
3 of 3 tests failed:

1) exchange buy should add a BUY nockmarket order:
   ReferenceError: exchange is not defined
```

Once you have all the tests failing—congratulations! You are ready to move on to the next step.

Does it feel strange to be congratulated for the tests failing? Is it even stranger to have done all this work without actually having written a single line of business logic? Numerous studies have shown that bugs caught later in the development cycle are exponentially more costly and difficult to fix. The small inconvenience of testing early will save you the larger one of digging through thousands of lines of code to find an obscure bug—one that potentially could have been detected before a single line of application code was written. Remember: test early and test often!

Building the Exchange

Now that we have prepared our unit tests, it gives us a fair degree of insight into what's required for the implementation. Let's start with the exchange data. How should this be structured? Intuitively, the order book is split into "buys" and "sells," so this seems like a logical place to start. The buy and sell side both have orders, each with a price and a volume, so this is another reasonable division. In JSON, this would resemble the following:

```
exchangeData: {
  buys: {prices: ..., volumes: ...}
  sells: {prices: ..., volumes: ...}
}
```

 JavaScript Object Notation

Created by Douglas Crockford, **JSON** stands for JavaScript Object Notation.[4] While derived from the JavaScript syntax, it is very widely used as an all-purpose data exchange format. It's rapidly becoming the *lingua franca* for data interchange over the Web[5] and is adopted by titans of the industry such as Facebook and Twitter.

---

[4] https://developer.mozilla.org/en-US/docs/JSON
[5] https://dev.twitter.com/docs/twitter-ids-json-and-snowflake

Now that we have an idea of what the data should look like, we now need to choose data structures for the implementation. To store volumes, we'll use a simple JSON object. This data structure is analogous to a hash table in other programming languages, and will allow for near-constant lookup time. In other words, the time taken to retrieve an element remains roughly the same as the size of the data structure grows. To store prices, I have adapted Marijn Haverbeke's binary heap. No need for me to go into the technical details of the implementing a binary heap because Marijn does an excellent job in his online book.[6]

 Objects as Hash Tables

Guillermo Rauch has written an article about some of the pitfalls of using an object as a hash.[7] The main danger lies in potential collisions that can occur when users are allowed to provide arbitrary input. This does not apply in our case because the inputs to the object are strictly under our control.

We will make two small modifications. First, we allow the user to pass a flag indicating whether the heap is maximum or minimum (that is, whether it starts at the largest value or smallest value). This is done by transforming the original code:

```
this.content.push(element);
```

... into the following:

```
if (this.options.max) {
   this.content.push(-element);
}
else
   this.content.push(element);
```

If users wish for a maximum heap, all that they need do is reverse the sign of the number. Internally, the data structure still finds the smallest number. However, the smallest negative number when examining negative values ends up being the largest when considering the absolute value.

---

[6] http://eloquentjavascript.net/appendix2.html
[7] http://www.devthought.com/2012/01/18/an-object-is-not-a-hash/

To illustrate, suppose we have 1, 4, and 10. The unmodified implementation returns the minimum number by default, which is 1. However, if we store the numbers internally as −1, −4 and −10, the smallest number now becomes −10.

All we need to do is remember to flip the sign back to a positive number before we return the result:

```
if (this.options.max)
  return -result;
else
  return result;
```

We require both maximum and minimum heaps because trades occur at the highest buy prices but the lowest sell prices. Our second modification is to add a peek function that works similarly to pop, except without removal:

```
peek: function() {
  if (this.options.max)
    return -this.content[0];
  else
    return this.content[0];
}
```

The peek function is simple. Internally, the data structure is an array, so all we need to do is return the first element of the array. We'll flip the sign if we're dealing with a maximum heap.

I will limit further observations to noting that with the addition of this data structure, JavaScript is starting to resemble much more closely some of the other languages you may have studied in Algorithms 101. Perhaps you can begin to see that it's not just a funny little language for browser manipulation.

Download the full code available at https://gist.github.com/3949948 and copy it into chapter02/lib/BinaryHeap.js.

The Heart of the Engine

JavaScript is a language that's generally read from top to bottom. This is also how we'll analyze the code for our trading engine, starting at the very first line. Unless otherwise noted, you can simply enter the following code in the exact same order

it appears in the text. The first part of the exchange engine, to be included in
lib/exchange.js, is as follows:

```
chapter02/lib/exchange.js (excerpt)

'use strict';

var $ = require('jquery') ❶
  , BinaryHeap = require('./BinaryHeap'); ❷

var BUY = "buys", SELL = "sells"; ❸

function createBinaryHeap(orderType) { ❹
  return new BinaryHeap(function (x) {
    return x;
  }, orderType);
}
```

❶   First, we import the jQuery library. Although jQuery is primarily a client-side
    library, we use it here for its clone function, which is discussed in more detail
    shortly. $ is the idiomatic way to refer to the jQuery library, and this is a con-
    vention to which we'll adhere.

❷   Next we import the binary heap ...

❸   ... and define some constants.

❹   Finally, we have a small helper function to create a new binary heap.

jQuery on the Server

One of the appeals of Node.js is the concept of "one language to rule them all."
In a perfect world, we would have seamless integration of client-side and server-
side code. As it currently stands, best practices are still emerging, and there is
still sometimes friction when bringing client code to the server and vice versa.

Bringing jQuery to the server is not a standard technique; some might even consider
it slightly unorthodox. I use it here to provide an example of what is possible.
You should experiment with various combinations to find out what works best
for your particular project.

Next, there is a function that takes existing exchange data and clones it:

chapter02/lib/exchange.js *(excerpt)*

```
function createExchange(exchangeData) {
  var cloned = $.extend(true, {}, exchangeData);
  cloned.trades = [];
  init(cloned, BUY);
  init(cloned, SELL);
  return cloned;

  function init(exchange, orderType) {
    if (!exchange[orderType]) {
      exchange[orderType] = {};
      exchange[orderType].volumes = {};
      var options = {};
      if (BUY == orderType) options.max = true;
      exchange[orderType].prices = createBinaryHeap(options);
    }
  }
}
```

This warrants further explanation. Why go to the trouble of cloning the data? Why not just manipulate it directly as we might do in object-oriented programming? In pure functional programming, functions have no side effects. This means that if you pass a parameter into a function, you expect it to emerge unchanged on the other side.

This makes a lot of sense. Imagine that you're using a public API and you feed it some data, which then appears mangled in the response. That piece of data is rendered effectively unusable because without knowing the internal workings of the API, it's difficult to work out what has changed.

That's why we clone the exchange data that has been passed in. If somebody wishes to use it subsequently in a different context, they can do so safe in the knowledge that their data has passed through untouched. Although the following does not apply to single-threaded JavaScript, immutable data also makes it easier to write multi-threaded applications because the data can be used by multiple threads, safe in the knowledge that its value will never change.

The Perils of Mutation

The native MongoDB driver for Node.js (to be discussed in Chapter 3) mutates inserted objects by adding an _id field. Most of the time this is fine; however, there are some edge cases where trouble can arise. For example, you will receive an error if you try to insert the same object twice. The first insert will work but the second one will complain about a duplicate ID.

It can be a source of confusion if you're unaware of the internal workings of the driver. In a purely functional language such as Haskell, this isn't an issue because you're guaranteed the value will never change. While it can sometimes be impractical to program in a purely functional style, I certainly encourage adopting its principles wherever possible.

The second interesting feature of the createExchange function code is that it contains another function called init. JavaScript allows for the declaration of functions within functions. Within init, we perform some basic initialization: if we receive empty exchange data, we set up an empty object to represent volumes and a new binary heap to indicate prices. As previously discussed, for buy orders we use a maximum binary heap because trades occur at the highest buy prices.

The Meat of the Problem

Now we'll build the core of the exchange. First, we'll set up some support functions:

chapter02/lib/exchange.js (excerpt)

```
    exchange[orderType].prices = createBinaryHeap(options);
  }
}
} module.exports = {
  BUY: BUY,
  SELL: SELL,
  buy:function (price, volume, exchangeData) {
    return order(BUY, price, volume, exchangeData);
  },
  sell:function (price, volume, exchangeData) {
    return order(SELL, price, volume, exchangeData);
  },
  order: order
}
```

module.exports is the Node.js syntax for exposing functions to other modules. BUY
and SELL are string constants, while buy and sell are thin wrappers around the
order function.

 Keep It DRY

> A naive implementation would be to write a buy function and then paste it to a
> sell function and change the necessary parts. You should never do this, as it
> violates the principle of **Don't Repeat Yourself (DRY)**. DRY is a programming
> philosophy that states that any piece of knowledge should have only a single
> representation. In simple terms, if you ever find yourself copying code from other
> places, there's a good chance you have violated DRY.

Note that module.exports is just a piece of JSON. While JSON is often used to
transport data, in this example we can see that it's also used to store function
definitions. This illustrates another important principle of functional programming:
functions are first-class citizens. Anywhere that you can use a variable, you can use
a function. If you start your REPL by typing node, you'll find this is perfectly legal:

```
var sayHello = function() {console.log('Hi');};
sayHello();
```

The Logical Core

Now we arrive at the most intricate piece of the puzzle: order processing. Let's add
the following to our **exchange.js** file:

chapter02/lib/exchange.js *(excerpt)*

```
function order(orderType, price, volume, exchangeData) {
  // Init
  var cloned = createExchange(exchangeData); ❶
  var orderBook = cloned[orderType]; ❷
  var oldVolume = orderBook.volumes[price]; ❸
```

❶ We begin the function with some initialization. First, we clone the data as ex-
    plained in the section called "The Heart of the Engine".

❷ The order book of the buy or sell transaction is then retrieved depending on
    orderType.

3 Finally, we retrieve all volume at the given price. `price` is converted into a string automatically.

Because `orderBook` is a JSON object, it can perform near-constant time lookups, and will be extremely fast. We use `oldVolume` to store the volume available at the specified price before processing the order.

Next, we determine whether a trade has occurred:

```
                                        chapter02/lib/exchange.js (excerpt)

⋮
function getOpposite() {
  return (BUY == orderType) ? SELL: BUY;
}
function isTrade() {
  var opp = cloned[getOpposite()].prices.peek();
  return (BUY == orderType) ? price >= opp : price <= opp;
}
var trade = isTrade();
```

First, we set up a small helper function, `getOpposite`. If it is a buy order, we return `SELL`, and vice versa.

 ## Closures

Notice how `getOpposite` "knows" about `orderType`, even though `orderType` was defined externally to that function? This is an example of a programming technique known as closures. Even though functional programming offers no support for the concept of objects, closures allow us to represent states. In this case, our function can use the order type even though it's not explicitly passed in as a parameter.

Following this, the logic for `isTrade` is simple. First, we obtain the maximum price. For the case of a buy order, a trade occurs when the price is greater than or equal to the smallest sell order. For example, if there's a new buy order at a price of $40, a trade will occur if there's any existing sell order at $40 or less. In the case of a sell order, a trade occurs when the price is less than or equal to the largest buy order. For instance, if there's a new sell order at a price of $40, a trade will occur if there's any existing buy order at $40 or more. We use our added `peek` function to determine the highest or lowest price depending on whether we're dealing with buys or sells.

Now we handle the case when there is a trade:

```
                                        chapter02/lib/exchange.js (excerpt)

⋮
var remainingVolume = volume;
var storePrice = true;

if (trade) {
  var oppBook = cloned[BUY]

  if (orderType == BUY)
    oppBook = cloned[SELL]
```

remainingVolume stores the remaining volume after the trade. If a trade removes an entire level of the order book, a new price will need to be stored and this is why we have storePrice.

Our first step is to store in oppBook the opposite side of the order book to the current order. This is because a buy order interacts with the sell side of the book, and vice versa. Then we have a while loop:

```
                                        chapter02/lib/exchange.js (excerpt)

⋮
while (remainingVolume > 0
    && Object.keys(oppBook.volumes).length > 0) {
      var bestOppPrice = oppBook.prices.peek();
      var bestOppVol = oppBook.volumes[bestOppPrice];
```

The while loop checks to see that there's still remaining volume, and that there are still orders on the other side of the book. We use Object.keys to return all the own enumerable properties in the object.[8] This lets us determine whether there are still orders remaining. If so, we fetch the best price and volume available.

There are now two possible cases for trading. We will illustrate with reference to the original example, where we have a buy order of 100 units at $40 sitting in the order book. The first case is too small to remove any levels of the order book. In our example, this means any sell order of 99 units or fewer, as it will still leave at least one unit remaining at $40:

---

[8] https://developer.mozilla.org/en-US/docs/JavaScript/Reference/Global_Objects/Object/keys

```
if (bestOppVol > remainingVolume) {
  cloned.trades.push({price:bestOppPrice
    , volume:remainingVolume}); ❶
  oppBook.volumes[bestOppPrice] =
    oppBook.volumes[bestOppPrice] - remainingVolume; ❷
  remainingVolume = 0; ❸
  storePrice = false; ❹
}
```

In this case, several things happen:

❶   There is a trade at the prevailing base price, so we create a trade object in JSON format and add it to the `trades` array.

❷   From the existing volume, we subtract the order volume.

❸   The submitted order is completely filled, so the volume is set back to zero.

❹   Lastly, the order is small enough for there to be zero price impact. Therefore, we set a Boolean so that we know that no prices need to be changed later.

In the second case, the order is large enough to remove at least one level on the opposite side. This means any sell order of 100 units or more in our example, which will completely consume the buy order of 100 units at $40, leaving 0 units remaining:

```
  else {
    if (bestOppVol == remainingVolume) ❶
      storePrice = false; ❷
    cloned.trades.push(
      {price:bestOppPrice
      , volume:oppBook.volumes[bestOppPrice]}); ❸
    remainingVolume =
      remainingVolume - oppBook.volumes[bestOppPrice]; ❹
    // Pop the best price from the heap
    oppBook.prices.pop(); ❺
    delete oppBook.volumes[bestOppPrice]; ❻
```

```
      }
    }
  }
}
```

① First, we need to test for the edge case where the incoming order volume matches the existing order volume exactly.

② In this case, the two orders will cancel each other out, so there's no need to store a new price.

③ Then, we generate the trade and push it into the `trades` array.

④ We adjust the volume by subtracting the entire amount of the volume on the opposite side. By way of example, if we had 100 units at $40 and a sell order came in for 130 units at $40, we would have 30 units remaining (130 - 100).

⑤ We then "pop" the price from the opposite side as it has been removed by the incoming order.

⑥ Similarly, we delete volume information from the opposite side.

Most of the hard work is done. Now we just need to clean up and return the data:

chapter02/lib/exchange.js (excerpt)

```
  ⋮
  if (!oldVolume && storePrice)
    cloned[orderType].prices.push(price);

  var newVolume = remainingVolume;

  // Add to existing volume
  if (oldVolume) newVolume += oldVolume;
  if (newVolume > 0)
    orderBook.volumes[price] = newVolume;
  return cloned;
}
```

Breaking it down step by step, if we need to store a new price, we do so:

```
if (!oldVolume && storePrice)
  cloned[orderType].prices.push(price);
```

If we need to store a new volume, we do the following:

```
var newVolume = remainingVolume;

// Add to existing volume
if (oldVolume) newVolume += oldVolume;
if (newVolume > 0)
  orderBook.volumes[price] = newVolume;
```

Lastly, we return all the data back from our function:

```
return cloned;
```

A Little More Action

So now we're done. Just kidding. What's the fun in building a stock exchange if there are no trades? In future chapters, we'll build a beautiful front-end interface to stream prices straight to the browser. For now, though, we'll present the data in plain old ASCII through the console. The first job is to add a rather mundane function that converts the order book to text.

Place the following function into your code, after `order: order` (with the comma):

chapter02/lib/exchange.js (excerpt)

```
order: order,

getDisplay: function(exchangeData) {
  var options = {max: true};
  var buyPrices = createBinaryHeap(options);
  var sellPrices = createBinaryHeap(options);
  var buys = exchangeData.buys;
  var sells = exchangeData.sells;

  if (sells) {
    for (var price in sells.volumes) {
      sellPrices.push(price);
    }
  }
  if (buys) {
    for (var price in buys.volumes) {
      buyPrices.push(price);
    }
```

```
    }

    var padding = "         | ";
    var stringBook = "\n";

    while (sellPrices.size() > 0) {
      var sellPrice = sellPrices.pop()
      stringBook +=
        padding + sellPrice + ", " + sells.volumes[sellPrice] + "\n";
    }
    while (buyPrices.size() > 0) {
      var buyPrice = buyPrices.pop();
      stringBook += buyPrice + ", " + buys.volumes[buyPrice] + "\n";
    }
    stringBook += "\n\n";
    for (var i=0; exchangeData.trades
      && i < exchangeData.trades.length; i++) {
        var trade = exchangeData.trades[i];
        stringBook +=
          "TRADE " + trade.volume + " @ " + trade.price + "\n";
    }
    return stringBook;
}
```

It is primarily an exercise in manipulating text on the screen with no interesting aspects to comment upon. Now within the **lib** directory, create **nocklib.js**:

chapter02/lib/nocklib.js *(excerpt)*

```
'use strict';

var exchange = require('./exchange')
  , priceFloor = 35
  , priceRange = 10
  , volFloor = 80
  , volRange = 40;

module.exports = {
  generateRandomOrder: function(exchangeData) {
    var order = {};
    if (Math.random() > 0.5) order.type = exchange.BUY
    else order.type = exchange.SELL

    var buyExists = exchangeData.buys
```

```
                         && exchangeData.buys.prices.peek();
    var sellExists = exchangeData.sells
                         && exchangeData.sells.prices.peek();
    var ran = Math.random();

    if (!buyExists && !sellExists)
      order.price = Math.floor(ran * priceRange) + priceFloor;
    else if (buyExists && sellExists) {
      if (Math.random() > 0.5)
        order.price = exchangeData.buys.prices.peek();
      else
        order.price = exchangeData.sells.prices.peek();
    } else if (buyExists) {
      order.price = exchangeData.buys.prices.peek();
    } else {
      order.price = exchangeData.sells.prices.peek();
    }

    var shift = Math.floor(Math.random() * priceRange / 2);

    if (Math.random() > 0.5) order.price += shift;
    else order.price -= shift;
    order.volume = Math.floor(Math.random() * volRange) + volFloor;
    return order;
  }
}
```

Here we're creating a library file, which at the moment contains only a single function to generate a random order. The logic is fairly simple. First, we randomly choose to buy or sell. If no data exists, we generate a price and volume according to prespecified ranges. Otherwise, we start at the best buy or sell price and shift the price randomly by a prespecified range before setting the volume.

At last, we can start firing orders into the exchange. In the root directory, place the following code into **nockmarket.js**:

chapter02/nockmarket.js *(excerpt)*

```
'use strict';

var exchangeData = {}
  , exch = require('./lib/exchange')
  , nocklib = require('./lib/nocklib')
```

```
  , timeFloor = 500
  , timeRange = 1000;

function submitRandomOrder() {
  // order
  var ord = nocklib.generateRandomOrder(exchangeData);
  console.log('order', ord);
  if (ord.type == exch.BUY)
    exchangeData = exch.buy(ord.price, ord.volume, exchangeData);
  else
    exchangeData = exch.sell(ord.price, ord.volume, exchangeData);

  var pause = Math.floor(Math.random() * timeRange) + timeFloor;
  setTimeout(submitRandomOrder, pause);
  console.log(exch.getDisplay(exchangeData));
}

submitRandomOrder();
```

First, we generate a random order and submit it to the exchange.

More on Asynchronous Programming

setTimeout as used here is a slightly more complicated example of the asynchronous programming model. What it does is pause for the specified amount of time before calling the specified function. In this case, we just call submitRandomOrder again, thereby creating an endless loop of orders.

If you now run node nockmarket, you should see an updating ASCII representation of the order book along with a printout of any trades. Once you have stared at it in fascination, we'll be ready to move on.

Oh, and what about those tests we wrote at the beginning? Go back to **exchange.test.js** and add a single line to your test cases:

chapter02/test/exchange.test.js *(excerpt)*

```
  , should = require('should')
  , exchange = require('../lib/exchange');
```

This will import the library we just wrote. Rerun make test and you should see in green something similar to the following:

```
3 tests complete (5ms)
```

In testing (just as in finance), green should rapidly become your favorite color.

What about the real thing?

I'm sure that some of you by now are wondering about real stock-market prices. Stock-market data is among the most interesting data in the world; unfortunately, the more interesting the data, the more expensive it is to access.

The freely available data that we're going to use is fairly pedestrian from both a finance and technology perspective. It's delayed data that contains only trade prices with no volume and no order information available. The example we've been building in this chapter, while simplified, still attempts to capture some of the richness of real-world markets. This leads to much more interesting learning opportunities, as we shall see in later chapters.

To prove how easy it is, we'll write a small module to retrieve real stock-market prices to finish off the chapter. The entire module can be written in 20 lines and is simple enough to analyze in one chunk. In the root directory, place the following into priceFeed.js:

chapter02/priceFeed.js

```javascript
var http = require('http');
var options = {
  host: 'download.finance.yahoo.com',
  port: 80,
  path: '/d/quotes.csv?s=AAPL,FB,GOOG,MSFT&f=s1c1d1&e=.csv'
};

http.get(options, function(res) {
  var data = '';
  res.on('data', function(chunk) {
    data += chunk.toString();
  })
  .on('error', function(err) {
    console.err('Error retrieving Yahoo stock prices');
    throw err;
  })
  .on('end', function() {
```

```
    console.log(data);
  });
});
```

First, we use the built-in `http` module. `options` is a JSON object, which we use to specify host, port, and path. When we receive a data event, we convert from raw bytes to a string as follows:

```
res.on('data', function(chunk) {
  data += chunk.toString();
})
```

If there is an error, we print the message and then throw the error. Finally, `'end'` indicates that all the data has been received, at which point we print the prices. On running the code (`node priceFeed.js`), you should receive rows of stock prices similar to the following:

```
"AAPL",582.10,+4.43,"6/22/2012"
```

We'll make more use of this data in subsequent chapters, but that's all for now.

Summary

In this chapter, you've learned the following:

- an introduction to test-driven development and basic should.js usage
- how to use the popular client-side jQuery library on the server
- how to employ `module.exports` and `require` to modularize your code
- `setTimeout` as an example of asynchronous programming
- first-class functions, functions within functions, and closures
- how server-side JavaScript can be used in conjunction with classical computer-science data structures and algorithms to build powerful programs
- implementing business logic—such as stock-exchange trading rules—in JavaScript
- how to use the native `http` module to retrieve real stock prices from Yahoo

Chapter 3

Persistence Pays

"Beware of bugs in the above code; I have only proved it correct, not tried it."

—Donald E. Knuth

Why MongoDB?

In this chapter, we'll learn to use MongoDB. MongoDB is a particular type of NoSQL database; specifically, it's a document-oriented database system. The Node.js ecosystem has excellent support for many popular relational database systems such as PostgreSQL and MySQL. Relational databases are robust and time-tested, and would adequately serve the needs of many modern-day web applications. So why are we using MongoDB? Let's now go over some of the main features of MongoDB to answer this question.

One of the most prominent features about MongoDB is that it is document-oriented and schema-free. The document referred to in **document-oriented** is a BSON document. This stands for Binary JSON,[1] which is conceptually similar to a JSON object

---

[1] http://bsonspec.org/

in JavaScript. **Schema-free** means that there's no predefined structure. A simple way to consider MongoDB is as a giant array of JSON objects with fast and powerful insertion and searching capabilities.

To a relational database purist, the concept of a schema-free database might be alien. However, there are certain use cases where MongoDB offers advantages over its relational counterpart.

First of all, it's well-suited to iterative development. Imagine we have a `Person` table and we wish to add a list of favorite movies. In a relational world, this would require an additional `Movie` table, and a joining table to store the relationships. In MongoDB, this could be done by simply adding an array of movies to the `Person` table, depending on the requirements. For a startup company with rapidly changing needs and an engineering team at capacity, the agility of MongoDB plays an important role.

MongoDB is also appropriate for unstructured data. In the world of finance, the derivative is a complex instrument; there are thousands of types (for example, futures, options, and swaps), each with unique properties. Capturing this in a relational database would pose a number of challenges, but using MongoDB it's as simple as representing the derivative in JSON and inserting it into the database. The derivatives can be of arbitrary complexity and sit side by side in a MongoDB collection.

Furthermore, MongoDB was designed from the ground up for big data, which is supported through a mechanism known as **sharding**. The conventional book form of the Yellow Pages[2] is a simple example, where it is typically divided into two shards, A-K and L-Z. Searching is faster because you simply choose the appropriate shard—a smaller volume of data. Conceptually, this is how sharding works with databases, though implementation is more complex.

Other use cases for MongoDB are discussed in detail on the official site.[3] In addition, MongoDB is quickly becoming the de facto database for Node.js. Jason Hoffman, founder of Joyent, has given a presentation on Node.js and MongoDB as a modern stack for the real-time web,[4] replacing the traditional LAMP (Linux, Apache, MySQL,

---

[2] http://www.yellowpages.com/

[3] http://www.mongodb.org/display/DOCS/Use+Cases

[4] http://www.10gen.com/presentations/mongosf-2012/n2m-nodejs-and-mongodb-as-the-modern-stack-for-the-real-time-web

PHP) stack. Once you begin building real-world projects, it's inevitable you will encounter MongoDB and use the skills acquired from this book.

Installation

We will switch from hosted MongoDB to a locally installed version. Installation is simple, and you can obtain the latest version from the following address: http://www.mongodb.org/downloads. Once you have the link for your specific platform, download and decompress the archive.

The following instructions work for Debian and Ubuntu systems. For other platforms, you can refer to the official documentation.[5] Your commands should resemble the following:

```
wget http://fastdl.mongodb.org/linux/mongodb-linux-x86_64-2.0.6.tgz

tar -xzvf mongodb-linux-x86_64-2.0.6.tgz
```

The only piece of configuration you have to do is to create **/data/db** as follows:

```
sudo mkdir /data

sudo mkdir /data/db
```

The last step is running the MongoDB daemon:

```
sudo mongodb-linux-x86_64-2.0.6/bin/mongod
```

If everything is successful, you should see the following (or similar) in the console:

```
:
[initandlisten] waiting for connections on port 27017
[websvr] admin web console waiting for connections on port 28017
```

Choosing the Driver

There are many MongoDB modules available for Node.js. The two most popular solutions are Mongoose and the native driver.

---

[5] http://www.mongodb.org/display/DOCS/Quickstart/

Mongoose is an object-to-document mapper, and was introduced briefly in Chapter 1. It provides a way of specifying schemas in Node.js, which are then translated into MongoDB BSON documents, and abstracts some of the lower-level implementation details. There is an advantage because the abstraction allows for rapid application development. The trade-off is decreased performance in certain situations due to all the wizardry happening behind the scenes.

The other option is the native driver, which is the officially supported driver from 10gen, the company behind MongoDB. The native driver forces you to deal with lower-level operations such as opening asynchronous database connections. You also need to determine how schemas should be handled at the application level.

There is a close correspondence between MongoDB operations and native driver operations, relieving developers of needing to learn too many idiosyncratic features. Additionally, it offers the best performance, as mentioned. Both drivers are excellent choices, but we'll use the native driver for the remainder of this book. Once you understand the basics of the native driver, it is relatively simple to switch across to Mongoose if this is a better fit for your business requirements.

A Quick Test

Our first objective for this chapter is to write a module that can:

- connect to MongoDB
- insert a business transaction
- retrieve a transaction

Let's begin the chapter with some unit tests, and extend what we built in the previous chapter. All the following instructions should be executed in the same directory that you've been using thus far. Place the following code into `test/db.test.js`:

chapter03/test/db.test.js (excerpt)

```
'use strict';

var assert = require('assert')
  , db = require('../lib/db')
  , nocklib = require('../lib/nocklib')
  , should = require('should');
```

```
var exchangeData = {};

suite('database', function() {
  var insertedOrder;

  test('open should open database connection', function(done) {
    db.open(done);
  });
  test('insertOne should insert a transaction', function(done) {
    var ord = nocklib.generateRandomOrder(exchangeData);
    db.insertOne('transactions', ord, function(err, order) {
      should.not.exist(err);
      should.exist(order._id);
      insertedOrder = order;
      done();
    });
  });
  test('findOne should find a single transaction', function(done) {
    var id = insertedOrder._id;
    db.findOne('transactions', id, function(err, order) {
      should.not.exist(err);
      should.exist(order._id);
      order.price.should.eql(insertedOrder.price);
      order.volume.should.eql(insertedOrder.volume);
      done();
    });
  });
});
```

Let's look at the main functions of that code. In the first test, we open up a connection to MongoDB. If this stage fails, all subsequent tests will fail, and so we'll know that a successful connection has yet to be established.

To insert an order, we first generate a random order using `generateRandomOrder` from Chapter 2. We then insert it into the database. Our main test is to check for for the existence of an `_id` field:

```
should.exist(order._id);
```

Object IDs

An Object ID is a field internally generated by MongoDB for every document in a collection. It is unique even across multiple machines. One handy feature is that the field contains an embedded date, so if you wish to know the creation date, a separate field is unnecessary.

To test our find function, we compare our randomly generated order to the order that has just been inserted into the database. We have found a successful match if price and volume are the same in the randomly generated order as they are in the newly inserted order:

```
order.price.should.eql(insertedOrder.price);
order.volume.should.eql(insertedOrder.volume);
```

Naming Your Fields

I encourage using expressive variable names. However, one particular quirk of MongoDB is that field names are repeated uncompressed in every single document. This means that if you have one million customer records with a field named isCustomerEligibleForDiscount, that field name is repeated a million times. Because there's no name compression, it's considered best practice to use shorter field names for collections that contain a large number of documents. Some companies use only one- to two-character field names in their collections.

Creating the Wrapper

Using the native driver directly in an application can be excessively verbose. That's why we'll create a thin wrapper around the native driver to abstract away some of the low-level details. First, we'll import some modules and run some setup code. Place the following into **lib/db.js**:

```
                                                   chapter03/lib/db.js (excerpt)

var Db = require('mongodb').Db
  ,Connection = require('mongodb').Connection
  ,Server = require('mongodb').Server;

var envHost = process.env['MONGO_NODE_DRIVER_HOST']
  ,envPort = process.env['MONGO_NODE_DRIVER_PORT']
```

```
  ,host = envHost != null ? envHost: 'localhost'
  ,port = envPort != null ? envPort: Connection.DEFAULT_PORT;

var db = new Db('nockmarket'
  ,new Server(host, port, {})
  ,{native_parser:false});
```

Most of the setup code is standard import and initialization. The one new item here is the process object, a way to interact with the native environment. It can perform operations such as changing directories, inspecting memory usage, and determining uptime.[6]

Here we use it to inspect environment variables, in particular hostname and port. In general, it's good practice to store configuration details such as hostnames, port names, usernames, and passwords outside of source code.

Imagine you have a production system and you wish to change the database port. If this is stored in source code, you'll need to change the source code and redeploy the system. In the meantime, a developer has sadly failed to follow a test-driven design and has introduced a bug into the system. This bug will be deployed into production just because we wanted to alter the port.

Some options for storing configuration details include:

- plain-text configuration files
- database storage
- environment variables

In all of these cases, it is possible to alter the configuration without modifying source code. For this example, we will ignore the environment variables, and therefore the host will default to localhost and the port will default to the default port.

Finding Data

Next, we'll create some functions for searching collections and add it to our code:

---

[6] http://nodejs.org/api/process.html

```
chapter03/lib/db.js (excerpt)
module.exports = {
  find: function(name, query, limit, callback) {
    db.collection(name).find(query)
      .sort({_id: -1})
      .limit(limit)
      .toArray(callback);
  },
  findOne: function(name, query, callback) {
    db.collection(name).findOne(query, callback);
  },
```

Here we implement two find functions. The first one finds all the documents matching a particular query. db.collection(name) selects the relevant collection. A collection is analogous to a table in relational database terminology. find is a function that executes the specified query. We'll delve into the specifics of the query language a little further on, but you'll probably be pleased to hear that syntactically it's based on JavaScript, which is one less hurdle to clear on your way to mastery.

After executing the query, we sort by _id in reverse order:

```
.sort({_id: -1})
```

This retrieves the newest entries first. We then apply a specified limit to avoid returning the entire database:

```
.limit(limit)
```

Lastly, we convert the result to an array and execute the callback function:

```
.toArray(callback);
```

Note how limit immediately follows sort, which immediately follows find. This technique is called **chaining**, and it provides a nice way to arbitrarily combine different operations.

findOne is very similar to find, except it will only return a single result; however, it's simpler because there's no requirement to sort, limit, or convert to an array. Generally, it is used to search by _id, which guarantees that there will only ever be a single match. If searching is performed on some other field and multiple matches arise, only the first match will be returned.

Inserting Data

Now we'll move on to the insertion functions:

chapter03/lib/db.js *(excerpt)*

```
insert: function(name, items, callback) {
  db.collection(name).insert(items, callback);
},
insertOne: function(name, item, callback) {
  module.exports.insert(name, item, function(err, items) {
    callback(err, items[0]);
  });
},
```

The `insert` function takes an array of items and inserts it into the database. The array consists of JSON objects, which can be of arbitrary form and have no correlation with objects that precede or follow. This illustrates the nature of schema-free databases well. If you wish to insert a financial transaction followed by an employee record followed by a chicken soup recipe, it is possible to do so (technically, at least). With MongoDB, the business rules that prevent this type of design are shifted away from the database system and towards the application.

`insertOne` is a thin wrapper around `insert` that calls the same function and returns the first item. It's a bit of **syntactic sugar**, a term describing code that's functionally identical to another piece of code but written in a more concise and elegant way.

In theory, `insertOne` is unnecessary and could always insert and retrieve single items by treating everything as an array of size one. This means that we'd access the result of the insert using syntax such as `result[0]`. It would be nicer to simply use the result because we know there will only be a single item. It may seem like a minor point, but over an entire code base, judicious use of syntactic sugar can add to the readability and maintainability of the code. Lastly, we add a small function that opens up the connection to the database:

```
                                           chapter03/lib/db.js (excerpt)

  open: function(callback) {
    db.open(callback);
  }
}
```

Our unit tests are now ready to run. Add the following dependencies to **package.json**:

```
                                         chapter03/package.json (excerpt)

{
  ⋮
  , "dependencies": {
    ⋮
    , "ejs" : "0.7.1"
    , "express": "2.5.8"
    , "mongodb": "1.0.2"
  }
}
```

After doing the customary `npm install` with the MongoDB daemon running, all the database unit tests should now pass upon running `make test`.

Storing the Data

Now that we have set up some scaffolding, we can modify **nockmarket.js** so that it stores orders in the database rather than just printing them to the console. The first modification is to open the connection to the database. To the list of imports, add `db = require('./lib/db')`. Replace the existing `submitRandomOrder` function call with the following:

```
                                        chapter03/nockmarket.js (excerpt)

db.open(function() {
  submitRandomOrder();
});
```

The main aspect to note about this code is the asynchronous style. We must ensure that the database is open before we can start placing orders.

Synchronous Code

Using the same excerpt, synchronous style code would resemble the following:

```
db.open();
submitRandomOrder();
```

In most languages, this is the standard way to handle interrelated functions; however, in JavaScript, this will end up submitting your order before opening a connection to the database because open is nonblocking.

Next, we modify our submit function as follows:

chapter03/nockmarket.js (excerpt)

```
function submitRandomOrder() {
  // order
  var ord = nocklib.generateRandomOrder(exchangeData);
  console.log('order', ord);
  if (ord.type == exch.BUY)
    exchangeData = exch.buy(ord.price, ord.volume, exchangeData);
  else
    exchangeData = exch.sell(ord.price, ord.volume, exchangeData);

  db.insertOne('transactions', ord, function(err, order) {
    if (exchangeData.trades && exchangeData.trades.length > 0) {
      var trades = exchangeData.trades.map(function(trade) {
        trade.init = (ord.type == exch.BUY) ? 'b' : 's';
        return trade;
      });
      db.insert('transactions', trades, function(err, trades) {
        pauseThenTrade();
      });
    }
    else pauseThenTrade();
  });

  function pauseThenTrade() {
    var pause = Math.floor(Math.random() * timeRange) + timeFloor;
    setTimeout(submitRandomOrder, pause);
    console.log(exch.getDisplay(exchangeData));
  }
}
```

The first new piece of code, `db.insertOne`, inserts our order into the database. Once the order is inserted and returned, we check to see if there have been any trades:

```
if (exchangeData.trades && exchangeData.trades.length > 0) {
```

If so, we use the built-in `map` function to add a flag indicating whether the trade was initiated by a buyer or a seller:

```
var trades = exchangeData.trades.map(function(trade) {
    trade.init = (ord.type == exch.BUY) ? 'b' : 's';
    return trade;
```

We are introducing this for two reasons. First, we want to demonstrate how easily MongoDB can handle heterogeneous documents. The introduction of an additional field adds complications to the relational database model. We have to either split the data into multiple tables, or else keep the data in a single table and have null fields and redundant data scattered across our data set. Neither is ideal. MongoDB does not need any workarounds and can naturally house different types of documents within the same collection.

The second reason for introducing this business rule is that it allows us to demonstrate the usage of `map`. The concept of map is to take a collection and transform it in some way. In this case, we use the built-in JavaScript `map` method and provide it with a transformation function that tells it how to transform an individual item in the collection.

 MapReduce

Map is part of a very powerful programming paradigm known as MapReduce. It wouldn't be an exaggeration to say that in many ways it forms the heart of Google's infrastructure. The official blog describes how Google use MapReduce to sort one petabyte of data.[7]

Depending on your particular programming background, the concept of map may not be immediately intuitive. Here's a basic example to help explain the concept. Start your read-eval-print (REPL) loop by typing `node`, and then the following line of code:

```
[1, 2, 3].map(function(x) { return x * 2; });
```

You should receive:

```
[ 2, 4, 6 ]
```

What this does is take the input array and apply a function to double each member of the array. To understand just how useful map is, I recommend trying to write functionally equivalent code without using map. You'll gain an appreciation for how it can be used to provide elegant solutions to transformation problems.

Before Express

Although we'll be primarily using Express.js to build our applications, it would be remiss to skip discussing the native http module briefly. As a short side project, we'll build a remote authentication module. The actual function will be physically located on a remote server, but can be called as if it were residing locally. This is possible because of a package called dnode, created by James Halliday.

First, add the following dependency to **package.json**: "dnode" : "1.0.0".

Now run npm install and then create a directory called **dnode**. Within the newly created **dnode** directory, create **auth.js**:

chapter03/dnode/auth.js *(excerpt)*

```
var dnode = require('dnode');
dnode(function(remote, conn) {
  this.auth = function(user, pass, cb) {
    var users = {
      foo: 'bar'
    };
    var p = users[user];
    if (p === pass) cb(null, 'AUTHORIZED!');
    else cb('REMOTE ACCESS DENIED');
  };
}).listen(process.argv[2]);
```

This defines a simple authentication function that does a lookup of the users JSON object (a production environment would look up the authentication details in an actual database). The authentication function is wrapped within the dnode function to make it accessible remotely.

Now we'll define the web server in the same folder, in **web.js**:

```
chapter03/dnode/web.js (excerpt)

var dnode = require('dnode')
  , http = require('http')
  , qs = require('querystring');

var d = dnode.connect('localhost', 8090);
d.on('remote', function (remote) {
  http.createServer(function(req, res) {
    if (req.url.match(/^\/login/)) {
      var param = qs.parse(req.url.split('?')[1]);
      remote.auth(param.user
        , param.pass, function (err, result) {
          res.end(err ? err: result);
      });
    }
  }).listen(process.argv[2]);
});
```

Once again, everything is wrapped in a dnode function to provide remote connectivity. The actual web server is created with http.createServer. We manually check the URL against a regular expression to determine if the user is trying to log in:

```
if (req.url.match(/^\/login/)) {
```

If so, we use the querystring built-in package to parse the username and password:

```
var param = qs.parse(req.url.split('?')[1]);
```

We then call the remote authentication function and render the result:

```
remote.auth(param.user
  , param.pass, function (err, result) {
    res.end(err ? err: result);
});
```

Run the authentication server using `node auth 8090` within the **dnode** folder, which starts the server and has it listen on port 8090. Then start the web server using `node web 3000`, and go to http://localhost:3000/login?user=foo&pass=bar in your browser. You should see the screen shown in Figure 3.1.

Figure 3.1. Consider yourself AUTHORIZED!

If you try to change the username or password in the address bar, you should see what's depicted in Figure 3.2.

Figure 3.2. When the user is unauthorized

In this case, we just happened to run the authentication server and web server on the same machine; however, the same code can be used for running a local web server with an authentication server on the other side of the world. The only change would be to specify the IP address of the remote server instead of using localhost. Now that we've built a basic web server using the native `http` module, it's time to build the rest of our application using Express.js.

Building an API

With some trades in our database, we will build a small API to retrieve the data. To be more specific, we'll build a **REST API**. REST stands for REpresentational State Transfer, which is the architecture behind the Web. Rather than discussing the technical details, it would be more illustrative to explain how the data moves from the database to the browser.

To begin with, the user makes a request to our Express server. From here within Express.js, we use the MongoDB native driver to make an asynchronous call to the database. Once the data is returned, we can manipulate it as desired to shift from the raw form to one that will be consumed by our API clients. Finally, we send the data back to the browser in JSON. Once the data returns to the browser, there are many applications and frameworks that can render the data in a way that's presentable to the user. We'll explore a way of doing this later in this chapter.

The first step is building the Express application. In Chapter 1, we did this using the command line. This added several lines of code, not all of which were explained or used. In this chapter, we'll construct the application line by line to give you a deeper sense of what we're doing and why. First, in **nockmarket.js**, import the express module as follows:

```
, express = require('express')
```

Then add the following just before `db.open`:

```
var app = express.createServer();
app.get('/', function(req, res) {
  res.send('Hello world');
});
```

Here we create the application and send the canonical "Hello world" whenever a user tries to access the base URL.

After that, modify the `db.open` function as follows:

```
db.open(function() {
  submitRandomOrder();  ❶
  app.listen(3000);  ❷
});
```

We only start listening for requests after we're sure the database is open. Now when you run node nockmarket with the MongoDB daemon running, two things should happen:

❶ As in Chapter 2, the program should generate and print random orders and the result. This time, the orders will also be stored in the database.

❷ A web server should start up, listening on port 3000. When you open in your browser http://localhost:3000, you should receive the "Hello world" greeting.

The second item is of limited interest in and of itself; however, we are about to make it more interesting by adding a new route, /api/trades, which will retrieve recent trades from the database. Enter this into **nockmarket.js**, just before db.open:

chapter03/nockmarket.js *(excerpt)*

```
app.get('/api/trades', function(req, res) {
  db.find('transactions'
    , {init: {$exists: true}}
    , 100, function(err, trades) {
    if (err) {
      console.error(err);
      return;
    }
    var json = [];
    var lastTime = 0;
    // Highstock expects an array of arrays. Each
    // subarray of form [time, price]
    trades.reverse().forEach(function(trade) {
      var date = new Date(parseInt(trade._id
        .toString()
        .substring(0,8), 16)*1000);
      var dataPoint = [date.getTime(), trade.price];
      if (date - lastTime > 1000)
        json.push(dataPoint);
      lastTime = date;
    });

    res.json(json);
  });
});
```

Let's step through it. The first line defines the route:

```
app.get('/api/trades', function(req, res) {
```

The next line defines the query that we perform on the database:

```
db.find('transactions'
  , {init: {$exists: true}}
  , 100, function(err, trades) {
```

Conveniently, MongoDB queries are in JSON format, so no new syntax has to be learned. The main concepts to learn are the MongoDB operations. Here, we're searching for documents where the `init` field exists. You'll recall that only trades have the `init` field. We limit the number of results to 100. For those familiar with SQL, there is an SQL-to-Mongo mapping chart available.[8]

Indexing

The query that we've presented will appear to run very quickly because of the data set's small size. In a production system, it would be essential to index certain fields to optimize search efficiency.

An everyday example of indexes is the Yellow Pages. If you look up a particular name, the alphabetical index enables a reasonably efficient search to find the desired entry rather than sequentially scanning from first page to last.

You only need to create an index once, and this can be done from a MongoDB shell completely outside of any Node.js environment. Indexing is a detailed topic, so for further information, a good source is the official documentation.[9]

The database extraction is now done. The rest of the function manipulates the returned array so that it's presented in the desired format for the charting application we're about to introduce. First, we reverse the array so that the timestamps appear in chronological order using `trades.reverse()`.

We use `forEach` to iterate over each element of the array. The graphical package that we'll be using expects data of the form `[time, price]`. We must first extract

---

[8] http://www.mongodb.org/display/DOCS/SQL+to+Mongo+Mapping+Chart
[9] http://www.mongodb.org/display/DOCS/Indexes

the time, which is conveniently embedded within _id. (Each MongoDB _id comes with an built-in timestamp.) We use a combination of .substring and parseInt to generate a JavaScript Date object.

Embedded Timestamps

The Object ID specification states that the first four bytes of an Object ID contain the timestamp.[10] To break down how this works, type node into your console and then the following:

```
var idString = '5015bd4d9d14890200000007';
```

This will store an ID in string format. You can copy the above verbatim or else use an ID directly from your own database. Then we extract the first four bytes:

```
var timestamp = idString.substring(0, 8);
```

Lastly, we parse the integer:

```
new Date(parseInt(timestamp, 16)*1000);
```

16 indicates that we're converting from hexadecimal, and we multiply by 1,000 to do a millisecond conversion. Your console should display similar to this:

```
Mon Jul 30 2012 08:46:37 GMT+1000 (EST)
```

We check to make sure that trades don't occur simultaneously. In the real world, multiple trades can happen at exactly the same instance at multiple price steps. In practice, this causes chart rendering issues. For simplicity, we will ensure a single trade for each timestamp.

Mind the Gap

The checking of simultaneous trades is purely a client-side check that we perform at the very last step. It doesn't affect the underlying data and so any portfolio calculations will be based on the correct data. We use this small workaround be-

---

[10] http://www.mongodb.org/display/DOCS/Object+IDs

cause the charting software fails to render simultaneous trades very well out of the box. Feel free to play around with the settings to see if you can come up with a better solution.

Last of all, we call `res.json` to stream the data to the client. If you now visit http://localhost:3000/api/trades, you should see output similar to the following:

```
[[1341838075000,58],[1341838078000,58],[1341838080000,57],
 ...[1341838240000,57],[1341838243000,59]]
```

Congratulations! You have now learned how to insert arbitrary documents into MongoDB, extract them using a simple query, and create a basic REST API to transform the data and present it back in JSON format—what Facebook and Twitter use to present data. For an example, visit https://graph.facebook.com/19292868552 and you should see what's in Figure 3.3.

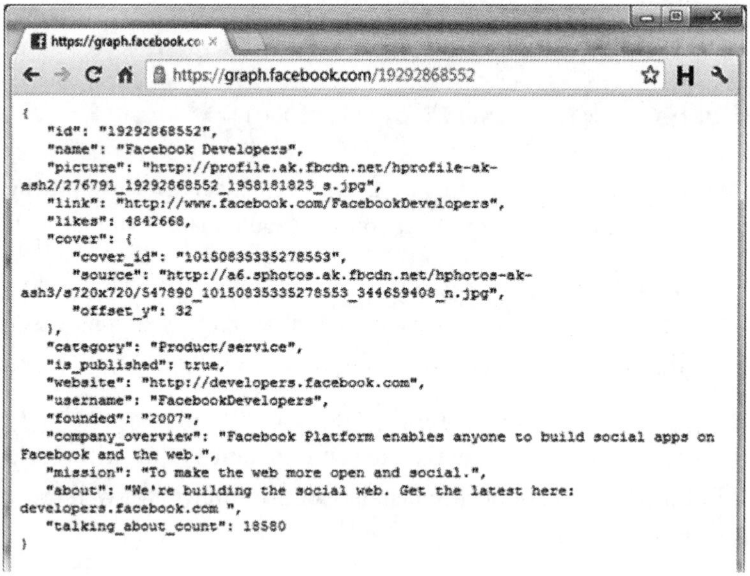

Figure 3.3. Sample Facebook data

If your application goes viral and you need to provide an API for other clients to access your data, you now understand the basics.

Charting the Result

We've now finished learning about MongoDB, but it's unsatisfying to only see the data in raw JSON format. There are many ways to present the results of JSON, and here we'll explore Highstock, a library built on jQuery and available at Highcharts.[11] Place the following just below the definition of app. It will be necessary to overwrite the previous "Hello world" code for the / route.

chapter03/nockmarket.js (excerpt)

```
var app = express.createServer();
app.configure(function () {
  app.set('views', __dirname + '/views');
  app.set('view engine', 'ejs');
  app.use(express.static(__dirname + '/public'));
});
app.set('view options', {
  layout: false
});
app.get('/', function(req, res) {
  res.render('chart');
});
```

In the configure function, we first define the template directory and then EJS (Embedded JavaScript) as the templating engine. By specifying layout: false, we indicate that no default layout is being used as a template. express.static is used to indicate the directory where we'll store static files such as stylesheets and images. Lastly, we modify the / route to display our chart template.

Paste the code from https://gist.github.com/3949958 into **/views/chart.ejs**.

Just about all the code is specifically related to the Highstock package, so I'll skip discussing it. It is primarily Highstock-specific configuration.

The final result should look like Figure 3.4 when you visit http://localhost:3000.

---

[11] http://highcharts.com

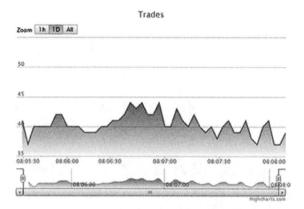

Figure 3.4. Visualizing our data

Congratulations, you have now mastered the basics of using MongoDB with Node.js. You now know how to insert and extract arbitrary JSON from MongoDB. You can construct a REST API that can be consumed by both internal and external clients. Finally, you have explored one way of presenting this data to end users.

Summary

In this chapter, we have covered the following:

- an introduction to MongoDB and what differentiates it from traditional relational database technology
- MongoDB installation and an overview of the two main drivers
- basic inserting, finding, and sorting
- using the native process object and http module
- using map to transform collections
- building a REST API
- presenting JSON data to the user

Beautifying with Bootstrap

"When you're a carpenter making a beautiful chest of drawers, you're not going to use a piece of plywood on the back, even though it faces the wall and nobody will ever see it. You'll know it's there, so you're going to use a beautiful piece of wood on the back. For you to sleep well at night, the aesthetic, the quality, has to be carried all the way through."

—Steve Jobs

Introduction

As a budding server-side engineer, your primary job is to make your application fast, make it work, and make it scalable. Making it pretty is generally outside of your job description. Nonetheless, there are now frameworks and toolkits available to make your web pages very presentable, even if they lack the final polish that a professional designer can provide. In this chapter, we'll introduce one such framework, Bootstrap,[1] an open-source project released by Twitter.

---

[1] http://twitter.github.com/bootstrap/

By the end of this chapter, you will have built a competent authentication system, which will supersede the toy systems we've built in prior chapters. After building a module that allows users to sign up and log in, we'll then create a module enabling users to add stocks to their portfolios. As icing on the cake, we'll retrieve live stock prices by adapting some of the code written in Chapter 2. Aside from learning about Bootstrap, we'll also build and extend upon some of the basic MongoDB skills acquired in Chapter 3.

Sign Up, Sign In

Our first task is to revisit the authentication module. Since you now know the basics of MongoDB, we'll be able to build a real module, instead of a mock one. Using Bootstrap, a basic well-designed web page is easy to construct. Once again, we will build on the work from the prior chapter. Modify **nockmarket.js** to replace the / route as follows:

chapter04/nockmarket.js *(excerpt)*

```
app.get('/', nockroutes.getIndex);
```

This looks a lot simpler than our previous routing code, and that's the intention. At the moment, our **nockmarket.js** does a few too many things: from setting up the Express.js server to doing order submissions to performing some business logic. Handling multiple roles in a single file works for simple applications, but quickly becomes unmanageable as complexity increases. Modularization is one of the keys to managing complexity, and here we will separate routing into another module.

It's time to introduce the concept of having separate, dedicated routing files. Create **routes/nockroutes.js** as follows:

chapter04/routes/nockroutes.js

```
module.exports = {
  getIndex: function(req, res) {
    res.render('index');
  }
}
```

Here we use the familiar `module.exports` to expose a function that renders the index template. To gain access to the routing file, we need an additional import in **nockmarket.js**:

chapter04/nockmarket.js *(excerpt)*

```
, nocklib = require('./lib/nocklib')
, nockroutes = require('./routes/nockroutes.js')
, timeFloor = 500
```

We can create the landing page by placing the following code into **index.ejs** within the **views** directory:

chapter04/views/index.ejs *(excerpt)*

```html
<!DOCTYPE html>
<html lang="en">
<head>
  <meta charset="utf-8">
  <title>Nockmarket</title>
  <meta name="viewport"
    content="width=device-width, initial-scale=1.0">
  <link href="http://twitter.github.com/bootstrap/assets/css/
➥bootstrap.css" rel="stylesheet">
  <link href="http://spbooks.github.com/nodejs1/docs.css"
    rel="stylesheet">
  <script src="http://twitter.github.com/bootstrap/assets/js/
➥google-code-prettify/prettify.js"></script>
</head>
<body>
<div class="container">
  <div class="marketing"><h1>Nockmarket</h1>
    <p class="marketing-byline">Welcome to the Node.js
      stockmarket</p>
    <div class="row offset2">
      <div class="span4"><img
        src="http://twitter.github.com/bootstrap/assets/img/
➥glyphicons/glyphicons_079_podium.png" class="bs-icon" alt="">
        <h2>Real Prices</h2>
        <p>Here you will be able to sign up for an account and
          create a stock portfolio with live prices. This will
          combine the beauty of Bootstrap with the performance of
          Node.js to create a well designed, blazing fast stock
          tracking tool.
```

```
        </p>
      </div>
      <div class="span4"><img
        src="http://twitter.github.com/bootstrap/assets/img/
➡glyphicons/glyphicons_266_book_open.png" class="bs-icon" alt="">
        <h2>Live Data</h2>
        <p>We will also construct a dummy portfolio to show you how
          to stream real-time data straight into your browser. Once
          you have mastered the basics you will be able to stream
          any type of data from tweets, to chat to auction data.
        </p>
      </div>
    </div>
  </div>
  <header class="jumbotron masthead">
    <div class="inner">
      <p class="download-info">
        <a data-toggle="modal" href="#" class="btn btn-large">Log In
          </a><a data-toggle="modal" href="#"
            class="btn btn-primary btn-large">Sign Up</a>
      </p>
    </div>
  </header>
</div>
</body>
</html>
```

There is nothing fancy about this code; it's just plain old HTML. We'll discuss some of the Bootstrap features later. Now when you run **node nockmarket** and go to http://localhost:3000, you should see the beautifully rendered page in Figure 4.1.

It's much better-looking than the plain vanilla forms we built in the first chapter! The effects you see are the result of hard work by the talented designers at Twitter following the principles of beautiful design. Bootstrap is a collection of well-designed widgets, plus some supporting JavaScript for added color. In the remainder of this chapter, we will see how we can combine this library with Node.js to build software that possesses both function and form.

Nockmarket

Welcome to the Node.js stockmarket

Real Prices

Here you will be able to sign up for an account and create a stock portfolio with live prices. This will combine the beauty of Bootstrap with the performance of Node.js to create a well designed, blazing fast start tracking tool.

Live Data

We will also construct a dummy portfolio to show you how to stream real-time data straight into your browser. Once you have mastered the basics you will be able to stream any type of data from tweets, to chat to auction data.

Log In   Sign Up

Figure 4.1. Our beautifully rendered landing page

The next step is to modify the code to incorporate some **modal windows**. Modals are the widgets that will allow users to enter their username and password. Bootstrap provides an implementation of modals, which includes both the front-end design and the associated JavaScript. We need to add the Bootstrap JavaScript code along with jQuery to **index.ejs**:

chapter04/views/index.ejs *(excerpt)*

```
<script src="http://twitter.github.com/bootstrap/assets/js/
➥google-code-prettify/prettify.js"></script>
  <script type="text/javascript" src="http://spbooks.github.com/
➥nodejs1/jquery.js"></script>
  <script type="text/javascript" src="http://spbooks.github.com/
➥nodejs1/bootstrap-button.js"></script>
  <script type="text/javascript" src="http://spbooks.github.com/
➥nodejs1/bootstrap-modal.js"></script>
  <script type="text/javascript" src="http://spbooks.github.com/
➥nodejs1/bootstrap-transition.js"></script>
</head>
```

Note that for better performance, you may combine and minify your Bootstrap files or use a content delivery network.[2] Next, we add some HTML code for the modal, which can be found at https://gist.github.com/3968474:[3]

---

[2] http://www.bootstrapcdn.com/

[3] For more details on modals, the Bootstrap site is an excellent reference [http://twitter.github.com/bootstrap/javascript.html#modals]

```
chapter04/views/index.ejs (excerpt)
<body>
<!-- paste code here -->
<div class="container">
```

Lastly, we make a small modification to `href` for our **Sign Up** button:

```
chapter04/views/index.ejs (excerpt)
<a data-toggle="modal" href="#myModal"
  class="btn btn-primary btn-large">Sign Up</a>
```

When you refresh the page and click on **Sign Up**, you should see a similar sight to Figure 4.2.

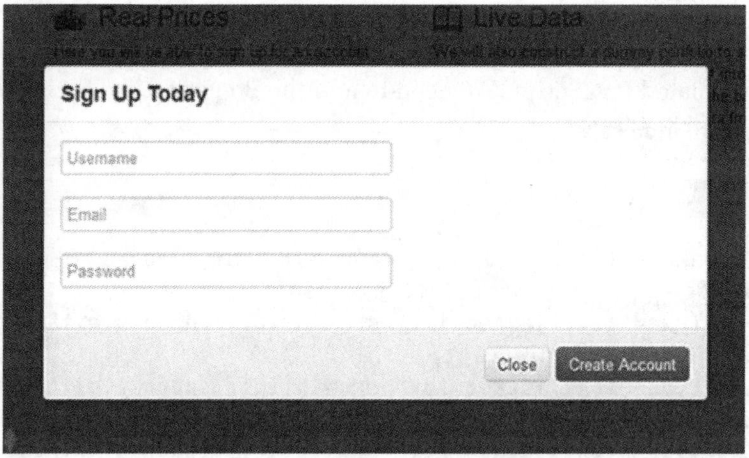

Figure 4.2. **Sign Up** modal

This concludes our whirlwind introduction to Bootstrap. For those who wish to investigate in further detail, w3resource has an in-depth explanation of all of the common widgets.[4] I hope now you can see how easy it is to construct a great-looking page. When we construct the user's stock portfolio section, we'll flesh out some of the key Bootstrap features in further detail. It's now time to implement some of the back-end functionality.

---

[4] http://www.w3resource.com/twitter-bootstrap/tutorial.php

A New User

Our first task is to add a line of configuration to **nockmarket.js** so that Express can parse form posts:

chapter04/nockmarket.js *(excerpt)*

```
app.configure(function () {
  app.use(express.bodyParser());
  app.set('views', __dirname + '/views');
  ⋮
});
```

Now let's modify **nocklib.js** by adding some functions to help us create a new user. First, we'll need some new imports to be able to encrypt the password and access our database library:

chapter04/lib/nocklib.js *(excerpt)*

```
var crypto = require('crypto')
  , db = require('./db')
  , exchange = require('./exchange')
```

Next, let's write a function to encrypt a plain-text password. Place the following below the `module.exports = { … }` code. It's unnecessary to expose this to other libraries because they do not require access to our encryption algorithm:

chapter04/lib/nocklib.js *(excerpt)*

```
function encryptPassword(plainText) {
  return crypto.createHash('md5').update(plainText).digest('hex');
}
```

Here, we're using the built-in `crypto` library. If some of the functions seem a little opaque, don't worry too much about it. Understanding what `createHash` and `digest` do behind the scenes is unimportant. For the perpetually curious, there is some detailed documentation of the crypto library on the official site.[5]

---

[5] http://nodejs.org/api/crypto.html

Robust Password Security

MD5 is generally considered a weak mechanism for storing passwords in production. bcrypt is a more secure alternative because it takes a lot longer to attack by brute force.[6] As you've come to expect, there is a package available for handling bcrypt encryption.[7] Because password functionality is encapsulated in a single function, it's easy to experiment with different hashing algorithms if you so desire.

Now let's write a function to access user data and import it into the database:

chapter04/lib/nocklib.js (excerpt)

```
module.exports = {
  createUser: function(username, email, password, callback) {
    var user = {username: username, email: email
      , password: encryptPassword(password)};
    db.insertOne('users', user, callback);
  },

  generateRandomOrder: function(exchangeData) {
```

Here we take the raw form inputs and construct a JSON object to represent the user. We never store the plain-text password; it is inserted into the database encrypted:

```
password: encryptPassword(password)
```

Finally, we use our insertOne function to insert a new user. This is almost identical to the way we insert new transactions. The only change is that we use a different collection name: users instead of transactions. We now need to add a route to **nockmarket.js** in order to accept form submissions from the browser:

chapter04/nockmarket.js (excerpt)

```
app.get('/', nockroutes.getIndex);
app.post('/signup', nockroutes.signup);
```

All we do here is define the route. The remainder of the routing code goes into **nockroutes.js**:

[6] http://codahale.com/how-to-safely-store-a-password/
[7] https://github.com/ncb000gt/node.bcrypt.jso

```
chapter04/routes/nockroutes.js (excerpt)

var nocklib = require('../lib/nocklib');

module.exports = {
  getIndex: function(req, res) {
    res.render('index');
  },
  signup: function(req, res) {
    nocklib.createUser(req.body.username
      , req.body.email
      , req.body.password, function(err, user) {
        console.log(user);
        res.redirect('/portfolio');
      });
  }
}
```

Remember the import of nocklib as the first line, and the comma after getIndex!
One more task is to remove the ASCII logging as this will no longer be required. In
nockmarket.js, comment out console.log(exch.getDisplay(exchangeData)); and
console.log('order', ord); with //. Both can be found within the function,
submitRandomOrder. Soon we'll be looking at much nicer ways to present the data.

Because we added the body parser earlier (using app.use(express.bodyParser())),
we can retrieve the form parameters using req.body.username, req.body.email,
and req.body.password. We then send these parameters to our createUser function.
I've included some logging so that you receive some feedback when the new user
is created. The last step redirects to **/portfolio.**

If you now restart the application and create a new user, you should see the following
or similar in your console:

```
{ username: 'nockuser',
  email: 'user@nockmarket.org',
  password: 'ebb080afaac3a990ad3f1d0f21742fac',
  _id: 501a16f5046680f873000003 }
```

We know that a user has been successfully created because the _id exists. It must
have been created by the database because we're unable to generate it ourselves.

Note that the password has been encrypted. You should be redirected to **/portfolio** with the message:

```
Cannot GET /portfolio
```

We'll be implementing this functionality a little later in the chapter.

There Can Be Only One

Users can now register on our website, but there is still one small problem. Duplicate registrations are allowed, which means that two unique users can end up with the same username. We'll now put in an Ajax check to inform the user whether their particular choice of username has already been taken.

 Why Ajax?

Ajax stands for Asynchronous JavaScript and XML. Ajax, via the `XMLHttpRequest` object, allows small pieces of information to be transmitted back and forth between a browser and a web server. Prior to this, even small changes to a page involved a full reload, leading to a sluggish user experience. Ajax enables a snappier, more responsive and interactive experience, as the following example demonstrates.

First, let's write a small library function to search by username. This can be done in a single line of business logic. Add the following to **nocklib.js**:

chapter04/lib/nocklib.js *(excerpt)*

```
  },

  getUser: function(username, callback) {
    db.findOne('users', {username: username}, callback);
  }
}
```

The query to search for a matching username is basic:

```
{username: username}
```

This query is in standard JSON syntax, which means that the left `username` refers to the field name and the right `username` refers to the variable. Once actual data is involved the query might resemble this: {username: 'johnsmith'}. We then add the associated routing. Append this route to **nockmarket.js**:

chapter04/nockmarket.js *(excerpt)*

```
app.get('/', nockroutes.getIndex);
app.get('/api/user/:username', nockroutes.getUser);
```

Note how a regular expression is used in the routing:

```
/api/user/:username
```

The :username portion means that we store anything after **/api/user/** in a variable called username. For example, if a person tries to access **/api/user/james**, the value 'james' will be stored inside req.params.username.

To complete the routing, add the following to **nockroutes.js**:

chapter04/routes/nockroutes.js *(excerpt)*

```
  },

  getUser: function(req, res) {
    nocklib.getUser(req.params.username, function(err, user) {
      if (user)
        res.send('1');
      else
        res.send('0');
    });
  },

  signup: function(req, res) {
```

Once we use this information in conjunction with our library to search for the user, the logic is simple. If the user exists, we send back '1' to indicate to the client that the user has been found. Otherwise, we send back '0'.

That's all we need for the back end. Our last effort is to connect it to the front end using jQuery. Import a new JavaScript source code file by editing **index.ejs**:

chapter04/views/index.ejs *(excerpt)*

```
<script type="text/javascript" src="http://spbooks.github.com/
➥nodejs1/bootstrap-transition.js"></script>
<script type="text/javascript" src="/js/nockclient.js"></script>
</head>
```

Create a new file called **nockclient.js** in **/public/js/** as follows:

chapter04/public/js/nockclient.js *(excerpt)*

```
$(document).ready(function() {
  $('.uname').blur(function(e) { ❶
    $.ajax({ ❷
      type: 'GET'
        , url: '/api/user/' + $('.uname').val()
    }).done(function(found) {
      if (found == '1') {
        $('#imagePlaceHolder')
          .html('<img src="http://spbooks.github.com/nodejs1/
➥cross.png" alt="cross"> Username already taken'); ❸
        $('.create-button').addClass('disabled')
          .attr('disabled', true); ❹
      }
      else {
        $('#imagePlaceHolder').html('<img src="http://spbooks
➥.github.com/nodejs1/tick.png" alt="tick">'); ❺
        $('.create-button').removeClass('disabled')
          .attr('disabled', false); ❻
      }
    });
  });
});
```

❶ The call to blur is triggered when the uname field loses focus.

❷ When this happens, we use the jQuery ajax function to fire a GET request to
our Node.js server.

❸ If the username is found, we display a cross to indicate that it's unavailable.

If you restart your server, click on **Sign Up**, and enter a username that's already
taken, you should see a similar sight to Figure 4.3 once the input loses focus.

④ We also disable the **Create Account** button so that the user is unable to submit the form with an invalid username.

⑤ If the username is available, we display a tick as in Figure 4.4.

⑥ Then we enable the **Create Account** button.

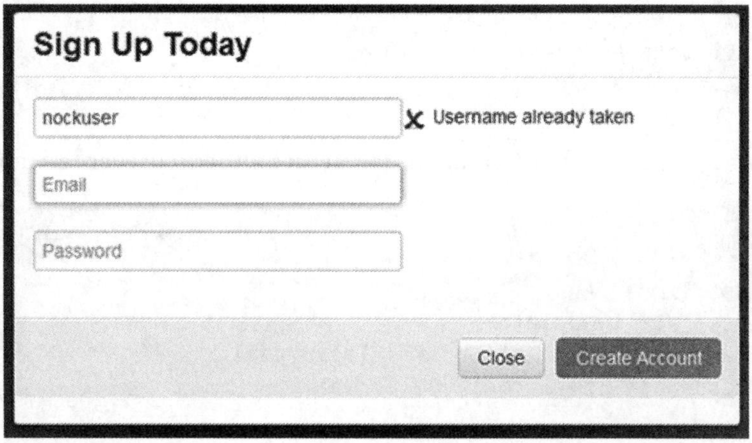

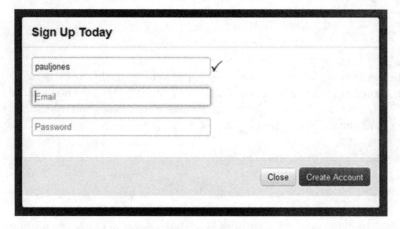

Figure 4.3. The username is invalid

Figure 4.4. Valid username

Go ahead and try the sign-up in your own browser, making sure the output resembles this. We have now completed the first part of the authentication process; namely, registering a new user. It's time to allow them to log in.

Authentication

Let's begin by modifying the front end to add a login modal. We construct the modal by including the code at https://gist.github.com/3968470 in **index.ejs**:

chapter04/views/index.ejs *(excerpt)*

```
</div>
<!-- paste code here -->
<div class="container">
```

We will now modify the href value for the login button to trigger the modal:

chapter04/views/index.ejs *(excerpt)*

```
<div class="inner">
  <p class="download-info">
    <a data-toggle="modal" href="#loginModal"
      class="btn btn-large">Log In</a>
```

As a quick check at this point, refresh the page and click on **Log In**. Now we can write a library function to authenticate the user. Add the following to **nocklib.js**:

chapter04/lib/nocklib.js *(excerpt)*

```
module.exports = {
  authenticate: function(username, password, callback) {
    db.findOne('users', {username: username}, function(err, user) {
      if (user && (user.password === encryptPassword(password))) ❶
        callback(err, user._id); ❷
      else
        callback(err, null); ❸
    });
  },
```

❶ Here we retrieve the user from the database. First we check whether the user exists, and then that the given password matches the encrypted password in the database.

❷ If there is a match, we return the ID.

❸ Otherwise we return null.

The reason we return the ID instead of simply `true` is because the user ID is a handy field that we'll utilize repeatedly. By returning it as part of the authentication function, we can save a separate call to the database further down the line.

The final step is to connect our library function to a route in **nockmarket.js**:

```
                                          chapter04/nockmarket.js (excerpt)

app.get('/api/user/:username', nockroutes.getUser);
app.post('/login', nockroutes.login);
```

We flesh out the body of the route in **nockroutes.js**:

```
                                    chapter04/routes/nockroutes.js (excerpt)

  },

  login: function(req, res) {
    nocklib.authenticate(req.body.username
      , req.body.password, function(err, id) {
        if (id) {
          res.redirect('/portfolio');
        }
        else
          res.redirect('/');
    });
  },

  signup: function(req, res) {
```

If the user is authenticated, we will redirect to the **/portfolio** page. If either the user does not exist or the passwords fail to match, we'll redirect to the home page. I'll leave it to you to redirect to a friendly error message in the case of failed authentication. At this point, you should have all the tools needed to accomplish this in a few lines of code.

There is one more task to do. Once the user has logged in, how do we keep track of that user in the future? One way is through the use of **sessions**, which is a way of storing information about the user on the server. This is in contrast to a cookie, which is used to store information about the user on the client device. Note that sessions may still use an HTTP cookie to store the session token. Therefore, cookies are required to store the session token even though other information is handled on the server side. We can configure Express.js with session support as follows:

chapter04/nockmarket.js (excerpt)

```
app.use(express.bodyParser());
app.use(express.cookieParser());
app.use(express.session({secret: 'secretpasswordforsessions'}));
```

This code will add support for sessions and cookies. Then when the user logs in, we can store the ID in the session variable. Modify **nockroutes.js** as follows:

chapter04/routes/nockroutes.js (excerpt)

```
if (id) {
  req.session._id = id;
  res.redirect('/portfolio');
```

Once the user ID has been stored, it can be accessed in the future using `req.session._id`. This will come in handy later when we use it to protect our portfolio page. It's now time to enable users to add stocks to their portfolios.

A Basic Portfolio

We'll now allow users to construct a basic portfolio. Let's begin by adding a library function that allows the user to retrieve an individual stock price. Inside **nocklib.js**, import the `http` module:

chapter04/lib/nocklib.js (excerpt)

```
, exchange = require('./exchange')
, http = require('http')
, priceFloor = 35
```

Then we make a small modification to the function we wrote in Chapter 2:

chapter04/lib/nocklib.js (excerpt)

```
},

getStockPrices: function(stocks, callback) {
  var stockList = '';
```

```
    stocks.forEach(function(stock) {
      stockList += stock + ',';
    });

    var options = {
      host: 'download.finance.yahoo.com',
      port: 80,
      path: '/d/quotes.csv?s=' + stockList + '&f=s1l1c1d1&e=.csv'
    };

    http.get(options, function(res) {
      var data = '';
      res.on('data', function(chunk) {
        data += chunk.toString();
      })
      .on('error', function(err) {
        console.err('Error retrieving Yahoo stock prices');
        throw err;
      })
      .on('end', function() {
        var tokens = data.split('\r\n');
        var prices = [];
        tokens.forEach(function(line) {
          var price = line.split(",")[1];
          if (price)
            prices.push(price);
          });
        callback(null, prices);
      });
    });
  },

getUser: function(username, callback)
```

The function is similar in that it uses the http module to retrieve prices from Yahoo. It first takes an array of stocks and converts it to a comma-delimited list:

```
stocks.forEach(function(stock) {
  stockList += stock + ',';
});
```

We then send this list to the Yahoo API, similar to what we did before. Upon getting the result, we parse the data and return an array:

```
var tokens = data.split('\r\n');
var prices = [];
tokens.forEach(function(line) {
  var price = line.split(",")[1];
  if (price)
    prices.push(price);
  });
callback(null, prices);
```

There is a one-to-one correspondence between the elements in the stock array and the elements in `prices`. Now we'll write a function that allows the user to add a stock to the portfolio. First, we'll amend our database wrapper by editing **lib/db.js**:

chapter04/lib/db.js (excerpt)

```
},
push: function(name, id, updateQuery, callback) {
  db.collection(name).update({_id: id}
    , {$push: updateQuery}, {safe:true}, callback);
}
}
```

We will represent the portfolio as an array of Strings within a `user` object. Here we're creating a generic function to allow the application to push data into an array. MongoDB's `update` function is combined with the $push modifier,[8] and we use `{safe:true}` to ensure that the callback is only fired once the item is inserted into the database. Without this, the callback function fires immediately.[9]

 Modifiers

MongoDB has a number of modifier operations that don't add any new function- ality as such. For instance, `$push` could be replicated by retrieving the object, manually pushing an item into an array, and then saving the entire object. What's handy about modifiers is that they can take place directly on the server, removing the overhead of sending an object from the database to the application and back again.

---

[8] http://www.mongodb.org/display/DOCS/Updating/#Updating-%24push
[9] http://mongodb.github.com/node-mongodb-native/markdown-docs/insert.html

Many I/O operations deal with events that are dependent upon each other. A typical example is to retrieve a user from the database based on ID and then look up stock prices in the user's stock portfolio. In these scenarios, the idiomatic Node.js technique for handling this is the **nested callback**, of which you've seen many examples. Nested callbacks take the following form:

```
getUser(id, function(err, user) {
  getPrices(user.stocks, function(err, prices) {
    // handle prices
  });
});
```

In this snippet, `getPrices` will always run after `getUser`. This is by design and it makes sense because we cannot know what prices to retrieve until the `user` object is returned from the database.

Suppose, however, that the events you're handling are independent, such as adding a stock to the portfolio and retrieving the stock price from Yahoo. When a user adds stock to the portfolio, two independent actions occur: we add stock to the portfolio using MongoDB, and we retrieve the stock price from Yahoo. Because of event independence, there's no need to run the events serially. We want to run the events in parallel. Therefore we don't want to use a nested callback.

Assume that adding stock to the portfolio takes one second, as does retrieving a price. Using a nested callback, the operation takes two seconds because the second action needs to wait for the first to complete before it can start. But if we were to run them in parallel, the total activity would only take one second to complete.

The issue is that we're unaware which event will finish first; so how do we determine where the callback should occur? There are a number of libraries that abstract away this complication; however, for this example, we'll avoid third-party libraries so that you can understand the principles behind what is happening. Let us define a new function within **nocklib.js**:

```
                                        chapter04/lib/nocklib.js (excerpt)

module.exports = {
  addStock: function(uid, stock, callback) {
    var price;
```

```
module.exports.getStockPrices([stock]
  , function(err, retrieved) {
    price = retrieved[0];
    doCallback();
});
db.push('users', new ObjectID(uid), {portfolio: stock}
  , doCallback);
},

authenticate: function(username, password, callback) {
```

Here we are defining a new function, addStock, which will add a specified stock to the user's portfolio.

There are two additional functions being called: push will add the stock to the user in the database, while getStockPrices will retrieve the stock price using the function we've just written. This function was written to handle multiple stocks, so it is trivial to use it to retrieve a single price by sending in an array of size one, and then retrieving the first element from the output.

We effectively make both calls at the same time, but without knowing which one will return first. This dilemma can be handled by having both events call the function doCallback, which we define here:

```
                                          chapter04/lib/nocklib.js (excerpt)

addStock: function(uid, stock, callback) {
  function doCallback() {
    counter++;
    if (counter == 2) {
      callback(null, price);
    }
  }

  var counter = 0;
```

We use the variable counter to keep track of how many times the callback function is called. In this way, it's of no consequence which function returns first. We always ignore the first call and return the price on the second call. There are libraries that elegantly abstract some of these details away; a good choice is async.[10]

---

[10] https://github.com/caolan/async/

Notice the use of `ObjectID` in our `addStock` function. It requires an additional import:

chapter04/lib/nocklib.js *(excerpt)*

```
, http = require('http')
, ObjectID = require('mongodb').ObjectID
```

To use MongoDB Object IDs, it is necessary to provide an actual `ObjectID` object. Avoid the mistake of sending in a different format such as a String, as this will fail to work. The final step is to add some routing to **nockmarket.js**:

chapter04/nockmarket.js *(excerpt)*

```
app.get('/api/user/:username', nockroutes.getUser);
app.post('/add-stock', nockroutes.addStock);
```

… and **nockroutes.js**:

chapter04/routes/nockroutes.js *(excerpt)*

```
module.exports = {
  addStock: function(req, res) {
    if (req.xhr) { ❶
      nocklib.addStock(req.session._id, req.body.stock
        , function(err, price) { ❷
          res.send(price); ❸
      });
    }
  },

  getIndex: function(req, res) {
```

❶ First, we check that the user is making an Ajax request.

❷ If so, we retrieve the ID from the session with `req.session._id` and the stock code from the HTTP POST with `req.body.stock`. Then we use our `addStock` function to add a stock to the portfolio and retrieve the price.

❸ Lastly, we send the price back to the browser.

The back end is now complete, so the next task is to connect it to the front end.

Bootstrap Widgets

Bootstrap comes with a variety of widgets, all of which have been meticulously crafted. Unfortunately, there's no time to cover all the different combinations in this book; however, once you have an example of how to integrate the Bootstrap widgets with Node.js, it's easy to take the principles and apply it to any widget. In this particular example, we'll use the tab interface. First, let's set up the head and body in **views/portfolio.ejs**:

chapter04/views/portfolio.ejs *(excerpt)*

```
<!DOCTYPE html>
<html lang="en">
<head>
  <meta charset="utf-8">
  <title>Nockmarket</title>
  <meta name="viewport"
    content="width=device-width, initial-scale=1.0">
  <link href="http://twitter.github.com/bootstrap/assets/css/
➥bootstrap.css" rel="stylesheet">
  <link href="http://spbooks.github.com/nodejs1/docs.css"
    rel="stylesheet">
  <script src="http://twitter.github.com/bootstrap/assets/js/
➥google-code-prettify/prettify.js"></script>
  <script type="text/javascript" src="http://spbooks.github.com/
➥nodejs1/jquery.js"></script>
  <script type="text/javascript" src="http://spbooks.github.com/
➥nodejs1/bootstrap-button.js"></script>
  <script type="text/javascript" src="http://spbooks.github.com/
➥nodejs1/bootstrap-modal.js"></script>
  <script type="text/javascript" src="http://spbooks.github.com/
➥nodejs1/bootstrap-transition.js"></script>
  <script type="text/javascript" src="http://twitter.github.com/
➥bootstrap/assets/js/bootstrap-tab.js"></script>
</head>
<body>
</body>
</html>
```

This code is likely to be very similar to any number of web pages you've set up in the past. Within the header, we load our CSS and JavaScript. We then have an empty body, which we begin to flesh out as follows:

chapter04/views/portfolio.ejs *(excerpt)*

```
<body>
  <div class="container">
    <div class="row">
    </div>
  </div>
</body>
```

From a design perspective, you can think of a Bootstrap web page as being composed of a series of rows. Each row consists of a number of columns; Bootstrap uses 12 columns by default. These can be constructed as follows:

chapter04/views/portfolio.ejs *(excerpt)*

```
<div class="row">
  <div class="offset2 span8">
  </div>
</div>
```

Here `offset2` specifies two empty columns. `span8` specifies that our actual content takes eight columns. In total, we have now specified 10 columns worth of content; the last two columns are empty. By having the same number of empty columns before and after our content, we ensure that the content is centered. The next step is to add the actual content from https://gist.github.com/3968465:

chapter04/views/portfolio.ejs *(excerpt)*

```
<div class="offset2 span8">
  <!-- paste code here -->
</div>
```

This step is as simple as taking the examples from the website and modifying the content accordingly. Then we define some simple routes in **nockmarket.js**:

chapter04/nockmarket.js *(excerpt)*

```
app.get('/api/user/:username', nockroutes.getUser);
app.get('/portfolio', nockroutes.portfolio);
```

As well as for **nockroutes.js**:

```
                                    chapter04/routes/nockroutes.js (excerpt)
},

portfolio: function(req, res) {
  res.render('portfolio');
},

login: function(req, res) {
```

Now when you log in, you should see a similar sight to that portrayed in Figure 4.5.

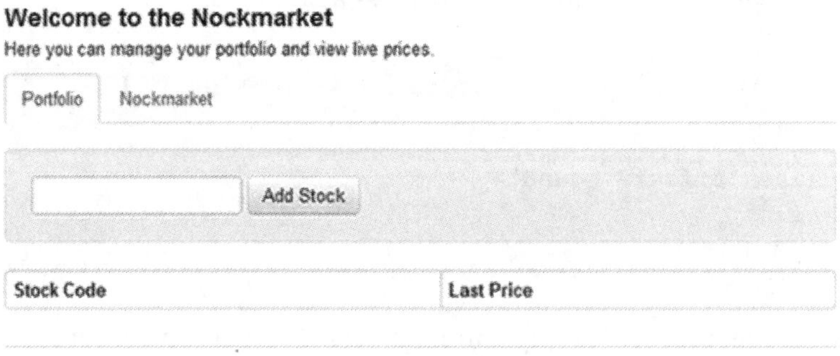

Welcome to the Nockmarket
Here you can manage your portfolio and view live prices.

Portfolio   Nockmarket

[   ]   Add Stock

Stock Code   Last Price

Figure 4.5. Time to diversify your portfolio

The tabs are functional so you can click between them, even if the current content is a little sparse. Now that we have our template, the last step is to write the front-end code to display added stocks with their prices. Let's start by adding our client-side JavaScript to **portfolio.ejs**:

```
                                    chapter04/views/portfolio.ejs (excerpt)
  <script type="text/javascript" src="http://twitter.github.com/
➥bootstrap/assets/js/bootstrap-tab.js"></script>
  <script type="text/javascript" src="/js/portfolio.js"></script>
</head>
```

Now create **/public/js/portfolio.js** as follows:

```
                                    chapter04/public/js/portfolio.js
$(document).ready(function() {
  $('#add-stock').click(function(e) {
    $.ajax({
```

```
    type: 'POST'
      , url: '/add-stock/'
      , data: {stock: $('#stock').val()}
  }).done(function(price) {
      $('.stock-list').append('<tr><td>' + $('#stock').val()
        + '</td><td>' + price + '</td></tr>');
  });
});
});
```

Here we use the jQuery's `ajax` function to submit a `POST` request to our Node.js server. Our server will return the stock price, at which point we manually append the data to our table:

```
$('.stock-list').append('<tr><td>' + $('#stock').val()
  + '</td><td>' + price + '</td></tr>');
```

This code is simply concatenating raw HTML with data. Although this is fine for simple issues, more complicated problems are best managed through a framework, one of which we'll explore in Chapter 6. Now as you begin adding stocks to your portfolio, you should have a view resembling Figure 4.6.

Welcome to the Nockmarket

Here you can manage your portfolio and view live prices.

Portfolio   Nockmarket

MSFT   Add Stock

Stock Code	Last Price
AAPL	621.70
DELL	12.41
GOOG	642.00
MSFT	30.42

Figure 4.6. Your portfolio with new stocks

The last task is to make the portfolio display when the page initially loads. Currently, if you refresh the page the stocks will no longer be displayed. First, we load the data in Node.js. Make the following modification in **nockroutes.js**:

chapter04/routes/nockroutes.js *(excerpt)*

```
portfolio: function(req, res) {
  nocklib.getUserById(req.session._id, function(err, user) {
    var portfolio = [];
    if (user && user.portfolio)
      portfolio = user.portfolio;
    nocklib.getStockPrices(portfolio, function(err, prices) {
      res.render('portfolio', {portfolio:portfolio, prices:prices});
    });
  });
},
```

Here we retrieve the user and then the stock prices for the user's portfolio. We send this into the template in two variables, portfolio and prices. This requires us to add getUserById in **nocklib.js**:

chapter04/lib/nocklib.js *(excerpt)*

```
getUserById: function(id, callback) {
  db.findOne('users', {_id: new ObjectID(id)}, callback);
},

getUser: function(username, callback) {
```

The getUserById function is similar to getUser, except that we search by _id instead of username. Then we display the data in a template. Make the following modification to **portfolio.ejs**:

chapter04/views/portfolio.ejs *(excerpt)*

```
<tbody class="stock-list">
  <% for (var i=0; i<portfolio.length; i++) { %>
    <tr><td><%=portfolio[i]%></td><td><%=prices[i]%></td></tr>
  <% } %>
</tbody>
```

We use a simple loop to display the data from the array, and the functionality is now complete. To finish, there is just one last piece to tidy up.

Password Protection

At the moment, the **/portfolio** route can be accessed by anybody. Express.js provides middleware functionality, which allows us to easily extend it with an access-checking mechanism. Define the following function in **nocklib.js**:

```
                                            chapter04/lib/nocklib.js (excerpt)

  },

  ensureAuthenticated: function (req, res, next) {
    if (req.session._id) {
      return next();
    }
    res.redirect('/');
  },

  generateRandomOrder: function(exchangeData) {
```

When the user first logs in, we store the ID in the session, which means that we check if the `_id` variable exists. If so, we know that we have a logged-in user and the `next` function tells Express.js to proceed as normal. If `_id` does not exist, we have a guest user whom we redirect back to the home page.

In this function, we can perform checks of arbitrary complexity. For example, rather than just checking for the existence of `_id`, we could retrieve the entire user profile and ensure that administrator rights exist before giving access to admin pages.

Protecting the page is now ridiculously easy:

```
                                            chapter04/nockmarket.js (excerpt)

app.get('/portfolio', nocklib.ensureAuthenticated,
  nockroutes.portfolio);
```

Note how `nocklib.ensureAuthenticated` appears to have been inserted into the middle of `get`. This feature of Express.js allows it to be extensible and flexible. Now if you try to access **/portfolio** without being signed in, you will be redirected to the home page.

Summary

In this chapter, we've covered the following:

- a basic introduction to Bootstrap widgets
- implementing a production authentication system and integrating this with Bootstrap login and sign-up modals
- providing faster and more interactive experiences through Ajax
- storing user data via sessions
- using the Bootstrap-tabbed interface to represent a stock portfolio
- dynamically adding and displaying stocks to the portfolio along with live prices
- access control using Express.js middleware

Chapter **5**

The Real-time Web

> "If everything seems under control, you're not going fast enough."
> —Mario Andretti

Welcome to arguably the most important chapter in the book. Here we will learn the basics of building a real-time chat website. This is made easy thanks to a package called Socket.IO,[1] or, if you like, "jQuery for sockets." What this means is you only have to learn the Socket.IO API. Under the hood, the API might be using WebSockets, Flash, Comet, and, in the future, technology that is yet to exist! Socket.IO will seamlessly change protocols depending on the user's browser capabilities without you having to write any additional code.

By the end of this chapter, you'll have written a real-time chat application with the ability to detect connecting and disconnecting users. You will have also connected Socket.IO to the stock-market simulator we built in Chapter 2 to stream real-time trades to a browser. Lastly, you'll have seen how Socket.IO can be used as a replacement for Ajax and traditional forms.

---

[1] http://socket.io/

Let's Chat

Enter WebSocket.[2] In the words of the author, "The goal … is to provide a mechanism for browser-based applications that need two-way communication with servers that does not rely on opening multiple HTTP connections (for example, using `<iframe>`s or `XMLHttpRequest` and long polling)."

WebSocket is a modern, bidirectional protocol that enables an interactive communication session between the browser and a server. Its main current drawback is that implementation is generally only available in the latest browsers. However, by using Socket.IO, this low level detail is abstracted away and you, as the programmer, are relieved of the need to write browser-specific code. Let us now see how we can incorporate this technology into our application.

We'll begin by building the prototypical chat application. Perhaps our users will wish to discuss with each other the merits of including more Apple stock in their portfolios, or the implications of the latest Federal Reserve meeting. Almost everybody is introduced to Socket.IO through a basic chat application. Although there are numerous examples of how to build such an application in very few lines of code, most of them are simplified, as they request that the user enter a display name. This removes the complication of connecting Socket.IO to an authorization system, which we'll actually be learning how to do.

Socket.IO is platform-agnostic and without built-in support for Express.js. There is some work involved in allowing Socket.IO access to the user ID session variable that we stored in Chapter 4. However, this step is crucial in using Socket.IO in a real-world environment.

Let's begin with an easier problem: building a front-end interface with our newly acquired Bootstrap skills. First, let's modify **portfolio.ejs** to add a new **Chat** tab:

chapter05/views/portfolio.ejs *(excerpt)*

```
<li><a href="#tab2" data-toggle="tab">Nockmarket</a></li>
<li><a href="#tab3" data-toggle="tab" id="chat-tab">Chat</a></li>
```

[2] http://tools.ietf.org/html/rfc6455

We can flesh out the content with a basic `textarea` to display conversations, an `input` field to enter text, and a `button` to submit chat messages:

```
                                              chapter05/views/portfolio.ejs (excerpt)
<div class="tab-pane" id="tab2">
  <p>Howdy, I'm in Section 2.</p>
</div>
<div class="tab-pane" id="tab3">
  <p><textarea class="input-xlarge span8 chat-widget" id="textarea"
    rows="20"></textarea></p>
  <p><input type="text" class="input-xlarge span8 chat-widget"
    id="input01" placeholder="Enter your message"></p>
  <p><button type="submit" class="btn btn-primary chat-widget"
    id="send-chat">Send</button></p>
</div>
```

The result is seen in Figure 5.1.

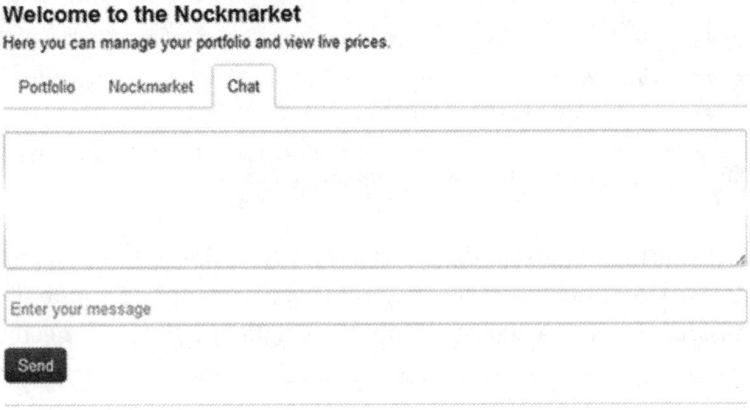

Figure 5.1. Ready to chat

Chat Tab Connecting Express with Socket.IO

So far, we have been accessing session variables by using `req.session._id`. `req` represents the HTTP request object. While Node.js uses this natively to communicate with the browser, Socket.IO works by sending and receiving custom messages between client and server. For example, the browser might send a "set nickname" message to the server, which would be handled as follows:

```
socket.on('set nickname', function (name) {
  ⋮
});
```

Note how in this code there is no direct access to the HTTP request object. Therefore, we require some mechanism for storing session variables. Accessing session variables is generally read-intensive since the session key must be decoded with every HTTP request. For maximum speed, best practice involves a purely in-memory solution, since reading and writing from RAM is much faster than doing so from disk.

A robust production setup would involve a database such as Redis [http://redis.io/]. Redis is a scalable, in-memory database system well-suited for this type of task. For an introductory text, it would be excessive to ask you to install and configure two database systems. Instead, we'll use the built-in `MemoryStore` for storing session information. Create a function in `nocklib.js` as follows:

chapter05/lib/nocklib.js *(excerpt)*

```
getSessionStore: function() {
  return sessionStore;
},

getStockPrices: function(stocks, callback) {
```

Because we're abstracting away the session functionality into a single function, if you wish to explore it further, it will be quite easy to switch to a more industrial-strength session storage mechanism. Only the single function will need to be changed; the rest of the code can remain intact. For a good starting point, have a look at Connect Redis [https://github.com/visionmedia/connect-redis]. To use `MemoryStore`, we introduce some additional imports into `nocklib.js`:

chapter05/lib/nocklib.js *(excerpt)*

```
, db = require('./db')
, exchange = require('./exchange')
, express = require('express')
, http = require('http')
, MemoryStore = express.session.MemoryStore
, ObjectID = require('mongodb').ObjectID
```

Once the imports are defined, a session storage object can be created as follows:

```
chapter05/lib/nocklib.js (excerpt)
```

```
, volRange = 40;

var sessionStore = new MemoryStore();
```

We will be using the `sessionStore` object as an intermediary to shuffle data back and forth between Express.js and Socket.IO. The last step is to modify `nockmarket.js` to configure Express to use session storage:

```
chapter05/nockmarket.js (excerpt)
```

```
app.use(express.session({secret: 'secretpasswordforsessions', store:
    nocklib.getSessionStore()}));
```

MemoryStore for Session Storage

MemoryStore is recommended more for prototyping than for production. Because memory storage ties user information to a specific machine, it limits flexibility when an application becomes big enough to scale out to several machines. A production configuration would use a more robust mechanism, such as the aforementioned Redis.

Now that we have a session storage mechanism, we can connect it with Socket.IO. First we add the dependency to **package.json**:

```
chapter05/package.json (excerpt)
```

```
, "should": "1.0.0"
, "socket.io": "0.9.10"
```

You will need to run the customary `npm install`. Let's now add a function in **nocklib.js** to create and configure a socket:

```
chapter05/lib/nocklib.js (excerpt)
```

```
},

createSocket: function(app) {
  io = require('socket.io').listen(app);
  io.configure(function (){
    io.set('authorization', function (handshakeData, callback) {
```

```
    });
  });
},

createUser: function(username, email, password, callback) {
```

Our function takes the Express app as a parameter, which is then passed into
Socket.IO's `listen` function.

Declare `io` as a variable at the top of **nocklib.js** as follows:

```
var sessionStore = new MemoryStore();
var io;
```

Call the `configure` function and begin by specifying the authorization procedure:

```
io.set('authorization', function (handshakeData, callback) {
  if (handshakeData.headers.cookie) {
    handshakeData.cookie = cookie
      .parse(decodeURIComponent(handshakeData.headers.cookie)); ❶
    handshakeData.sessionID = handshakeData.cookie['connect.sid'];
    sessionStore.get(handshakeData.sessionID
      , function (err, session) { ❷
        if (err || !session) {
          return callback(null, false); ❸
        } else {
          handshakeData.session = session;
          console.log('session data', session);
          return callback(null, true); ❹
        }
    });
  }
  else {
    return callback(null, false); ❺
  }
```

❶ The Socket.IO authorization mechanism comes with handshake data, which in turn comes with header data.[3] The header data will contain embedded cookie information, and it is here that we will find the encrypted session ID. This line will produce raw data similar to:

```
connect.sid=CGHs801f32T7Vc4VqSKszgjH.TryCeIqQjAGH6DvvjX6PweNK …
```

❷ We extract the session ID and then retrieve from our session store the actual session corresponding to the specified ID.

❸ We return the session—if we find it—to indicate successful authorization.

❹ If not, we return `false`.

❺ Lastly, we handle the case where no cookie is found.

The `configuration` function will require an additional import, dependency, and `npm install`. Here's the import:

chapter05/lib/nocklib.js *(excerpt)*

```
var cookie = require('cookie')
  , crypto = require('crypto')
```

… And the dependency:

chapter05/package.json *(excerpt)*

```
, "cookie": "0.0.4"
,"dnode" : "1.0.0"
```

There's one final tweak to **nockmarket.js** before back-end authorization is complete:

chapter05/nockmarket.js *(excerpt)*

```
db.open(function() {
  nocklib.createSocket(app);
  submitRandomOrder();
```

---

[3] https://github.com/LearnBoost/socket.io/wiki/Authorizing

Client Chat Code

Now we need to make a few changes to the client to see authorization in action. Add the following imports to **portfolio.ejs**:

```
                                        chapter05/views/portfolio.ejs (excerpt)

  <script src="/socket.io/socket.io.js"></script>
  <script src="/js/chat.js"></script>
</head>
```

The first included script is the Socket.IO client library. The second script is our custom chat library, which we'll now define. Create **/public/js/chat.js** as follows:

```
                                        chapter05/public/js/chat.js (excerpt)

var socket = io.connect('http://localhost');
```

For now, we just need a single line. If you restart and sign in, you should see in your console a similar sight to this:

```
session data { lastAccess: 1345420544817,
  cookie:
    { originalMaxAge: 14400000,
      expires: '2012-08-20T03:55:44.821Z',
      httpOnly: true,
      path: '/' },
  _id: '501ef76dfbd51a082d000001' }
```

In our code, we print out all the session information. This has data such as the cookie expiry, path, and the all-important _id field, which allows us to reliably match each request with a specified user in our database.

We'll now move on to doing something interesting with this field: having our users chat to each other in real time.

Who has joined?

Let's begin with the simplest possible component: a notification message when users have joined. Because username will be very handy, modify **routes/nockroutes.js** to store the username straight into the session upon signing in:

chapter05/routes/nockroutes.js *(excerpt)*

```
req.session._id = id;
req.session.username = req.body.username;
```

Now modify **nocklib.js** as follows:

chapter05/lib/nocklib.js *(excerpt)*

```
io.set('authorization', function (handshakeData, callback) {
  ⋮
});
io.sockets.on('connection', function (socket) {
  socket.on('joined', function (data) { ❶
    var message = 'Admin: ' + socket.handshake.session.username
      + ' has joined\n';
    socket.emit('chat', { message: message}); ❷
    socket.broadcast.emit('chat', { message: message}); ❸
  });
});
```

❶ First, we listen for a `'joined'` message to be emitted from the client.

❷ After constructing a message, we first send it to the user who initiated the `'joined'` message.

❸ Then we send a message to all the other users.

That's everything for the server side. On the client side, let's have a button that the user can press to join the chat room. Modify **portfolio.ejs** as follows:

chapter05/views/portfolio.ejs *(excerpt)*

```
<div class="tab-pane" id="tab3">
  <p><button class="btn btn-info btn-large btn-primary"
    type="button" id="join-chat">Join Chat</button></p>
```

After initially hiding all the chat widgets, we can show them while simultaneously emitting a `'joined'` message to the server when the user clicks on the **Join Chat** button. Modify **chat.js** as follows:

```
var socket = io.connect('http://localhost');
$(document).ready(function() {
  $('.chat-widget').hide();
  $('#join-chat').click(function() {
    $('#join-chat').hide();
    $('.chat-widget').show();
    socket.emit('joined', {});
  });
});
```

`socket.emit('joined', {});` sends a `'joined'` message to the server with no data, as indicated by {}. We've just finished writing the server code, which will process this message by emitting a `'chat'` message in reply. The `'chat'` message is then handled as follows:

```
$('#join-chat').click(function()  {
  ⋮
});
socket.on('chat', function (data) {
  $('#textarea').prepend(data.message);
});
```

We simply add the message to the existing textarea. Now make sure you have at least two users in the database. To simulate multiple users, sign in with each user from a separate browser. For example, one user might log in using Chrome, while the other user logs in using Firefox. When the second user logs in, you should see a similar sight to Figure 5.2 in the first browser once you've clicked 'Join Chat'.

Welcome to the Nockmarket

Here you can manage your portfolio and view live prices.

| Portfolio | Nockmarket | Chat |

```
Admin: sam has joined
Admin: paul has joined
```

Figure 5.2. Sam and Paul have joined the chat

Let Them Speak

From here it's quite simple to add the chat functionality. On the back end, we require just a few lines in **nocklib.js**:

chapter05/lib/nocklib.js *(excerpt)*

```
io.sockets.on('connection', function (socket) {
  socket.on('clientchat', function (data) {
    var message = socket.handshake.session.username + ': '
      + data.message + '\n';
    socket.emit('chat', { message: message});
    socket.broadcast.emit('chat', { message: message});
  });
```

This is similar to the code for a user joining the chat session. The main difference is we append the actual user chat data to the message. The chat data is accessed through `data.message`, which is transmitted by the client. The client side is also straightforward. Modify **chat.js** as follows:

chapter05/public/js/chat.js *(excerpt)*

```
  socket.emit('joined', {});
});
$('#send-chat').click(function() {
  socket.emit('clientchat', {message: $('#input01').val()});
});
```

When the user clicks the **Send** button, we grab the text from the `input` field and send a `'clientchat'` message to the server. It's that simple!

Now as you begin to enter messages and click **Send**, the chat messages should begin to appear in both windows simultaneously, as seen in Figure 5.3.

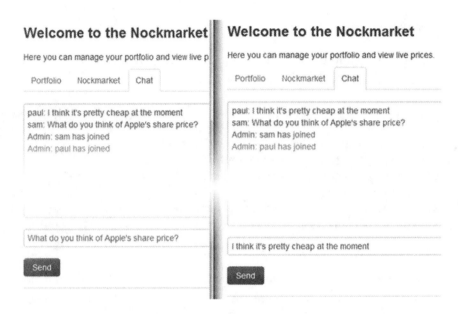

Figure 5.3. Simultaneous chat windows

Who's online?

Let's now use Socket.IO to detect online users. We will implement a feature to show the number of currently connected users along with their actual usernames. In **nocklib.js**, declare an array to store online users:

chapter05/lib/nocklib.js *(excerpt)*

```
var io;
var online = [];
```

Then we add some functionality to store the users and broadcast to connected clients:

chapter05/lib/nocklib.js *(excerpt)*

```
socket.on('joined', function (data) {
  online.push(socket.handshake.session.username);
  var message = socket.handshake.session.username + ': '
    + data.message + '\n';
  socket.emit('chat', { message: message
    , users: online});
  socket.broadcast.emit('chat', { message: message
    , username: socket.handshake.session.username});
```

If a new user connects, we add the username to the `online` array. Then we use `emit` to send the entire list of users to the one who has just connected. To everybody else, we broadcast a single user—the one who recently joined.

Then on the client side, modify **chat.js** as follows:

chapter05/public/js/chat.js (excerpt)

```
socket.on('chat', function (data) {
  $('#textarea').append(data.message);
  if (data.username) { ❶
    $('#users').append('<span class="label label-success">'
      + data.username + '</span>');
  }
  if (data.users) { ❷
    var userHtml = '';
    for (var i=0; i < data.users.length; i++) {
      userHtml += '<span class="label label-success">'
        + data.users[i] + '</span>';
    }
    $('#users').html(userHtml);
  }
});
```

❶ Here we apply some very simple logic. If the server sends down a single value, we append that user to the end of the existing list.

❷ If it sends down an array of users, we construct the list of users from scratch.

The final step is to modify **portfolio.ejs** by adding a placeholder to display our users:

chapter05/views/portfolio.ejs (excerpt)

```
<p><button type="submit" class="btn btn-primary chat-widget"
  id="send-chat">Send</button></p>
<p><span class="label label-inverse chat-widget"
  id="online">Online:</span><div id="users"></div></p>
```

Now if you sign in with one browser, and then sign in again under another name in another browser, the first browser should update in real time; that is, showing both users online, as in Figure 5.4.

Figure 5.4. Both Paul and Don are signed in and ready to roll

The last undertaking is to appropriately handle user disconnections. Socket.IO has a built-in disconnect mechanism for handling this. Add the following to **nocklib.js**:

```
                                              chapter05/lib/nocklib.js (excerpt)
socket.on('clientchat', function (data) {
  ⋮
});
socket.on('disconnect', function (data) {
  var username = socket.handshake.session.username;
  var index = online.indexOf(username);
  online.splice(index, 1); ❶
  socket.broadcast.emit('disconnect', { username: username}); ❷
});
```

When the user disconnects we do two things.

❶   First, we update the array containing all users to remove the disconnected user. We do this by finding the index of the user, and then employing JavaScript's built-in `splice` function.

❷   Second, we broadcast a `'disconnect'` message to all clients so that they can update the user interface appropriately.

Now we'll make a few small modifications to **chat.js**:

```
                                          chapter05/public/js/chat.js (excerpt)
if (data.username) {
  $('#users')
    .append('<span class="label label-success"
      id="username-' + data.username + '"
      >' + data.username + '</span>');
}
```

```
if (data.users) {
  var userHtml = '';
  for (var i=0; i<data.users.length; i++) {
    userHtml += '<span class="label label-success"
      id="username-' + data.users[i] + '"
      >' + data.users[i] + '</span>';
  }
  ⋮
```

For the first task, we have added some ids to our labels so that they can be identified and removed. The actual removal code is very simple:

chapter05/public/js/chat.js *(excerpt)*

```
    $('#users').html(userHtml);
  }
});
socket.on('disconnect', function (data) {
  $('#username-' + data.username).remove();
});
```

Upon receiving the 'disconnect' message, we search for the appropriate tag and perform a jQuery remove. Now as users disconnect, all the clients should update their interface in real time. To try this out, sign in as two unique users in separate browsers. Now close one of the browsers. The remaining browser should show an updated user list with the disconnected user removed.

Congratulations, you have just constructed a real-time, multi-user chat room! Your user base can now utilize it to discuss the latest minutes of the Federal Reserve or the earnings announcement of their favorite stock. Now it's time to use Socket.IO to send a very different kind of data: real-time trades.

Real-time Trades

We'll now build on the exchange we created in Chapter 2. Our ultimate goal is to send real-time financial data from the server to the browser. First, let's add some more stocks to the exchange. At the moment, it just trades in one hypothetical stock. Let's represent our stocks with an array of Strings. Modify **nockmarket.js** as follows:

```
  , timeRange = 1000;

var stocks = ['NOCK1', 'NOCK2', 'NOCK3', 'NOCK4', 'NOCK5'];
var allData = [];
stocks.forEach(function(stock) {allData.push({});});
```

Here we represent the stocks as an array containing Strings. We declare and initialize a corresponding array to hold the financial data for each stock. Then we make a few adjustments to `submitRandomOrder` so that it can accommodate multiple stocks:

```
function submitRandomOrder(index) {
  var exchangeData = allData[index];
  var ord = nocklib.generateRandomOrder(exchangeData);
  ord.stock = stocks[index];
  if (ord.type == exch.BUY)
    allData[index] = exch.buy(ord.price, ord.volume, exchangeData);
  else
    allData[index] = exch.sell(ord.price, ord.volume, exchangeData);
```

First, we add a parameter, `index`, to the function to represent which stock we're trading. Then, instead of using a single universal `exchangeData`, we use separate `exchangeData` for each stock. We now modify our order with a field `stock` to indicate which stock we're trading in:

```
var ord = nocklib.generateRandomOrder(exchangeData);
ord.stock = stocks[index];
```

This is as simple as it looks. We merely modify the JSON object; nothing else needs to change. MongoDB will seamlessly add the new field without us having to write any additional database-related code. This is similarly the case with trades:

```
trade.init = (ord.type == exch.BUY) ? 'b' : 's';
trade.stock = stocks[index];
```

We'll also modify our `pauseThenTrade` function as follows:

chapter05/nockmarket.js *(excerpt)*

```
function pauseThenTrade() {
  var pause = Math.floor(Math.random() * timeRange) + timeFloor;
  setTimeout(submitRandomOrder.bind(this, index), pause);
}
```

We now pass a parameter to `submitRandomOrder` to indicate which stock we're trading using JavaScript's `bind` mechanism. Sending trading data is perhaps the easiest code we've written in the entire book! Now add the following function to **nocklib.js** under your `getUser` function:

chapter05/lib/nocklib.js *(excerpt)*

```
  },

  sendTrades: function(trades) {
    io.sockets.emit('trade', JSON.stringify(trades));
  }
}
```

This function takes an array of trades and emits a `'trade'` message to all connected clients. `JSON.stringify` is purely for text formatting to make the data slightly easier to read. This is just a temporary measure; in Chapter 6, we'll make the data look more exciting than text in the console.

It's necessary to add one last line in **nockmarket.js** to send the trades:

chapter05/nockmarket.js *(excerpt)*

```
db.insertOne('transactions', ord, function(err, order) {
  if (exchangeData.trades && exchangeData.trades.length > 0) {
    nocklib.sendTrades(exchangeData.trades);
```

We'll also need to call `submitRandomOrder` once per stock:

```
                                    chapter05/nockmarket.js (excerpt)

nocklib.createSocket(app);
app.listen(3000);
for (var i = 0; i < stocks.length; i++) {
  submitRandomOrder(i);
}
```

Note that the existing `submitRandomOrder();` should be deleted. The server-side code is now complete.

Trades on the Client

For now, all we have to do on the client side is log the trades to confirm they are being successfully received. Add the following to **portfolio.ejs**:

```
                                 chapter05/views/portfolio.ejs (excerpt)

  <script src="/js/trades.js"></script>
</head>
```

Then create **/public/js/trades.js**:

```
                                      chapter05/public/js/trades.js

socket.on('trade', function (data) {
  console.log(data);
});
```

That's it! You'll have to be able to view your browser's console. The mechanism for doing this varies from browser to browser. In Chrome, you press **Ctrl-Shift-I** (**Cmd-Option-I** on a Mac). You may need to click the **Console** tab. Once you log in and open the console, you should see a view indicative of Figure 5.5.

```
[{"price":49,"volume":110,"init":"b","stock":"NOCK2"}]
[{"price":25,"volume":111,"init":"b","stock":"NOCK1"}]
[{"price":39,"volume":71,"init":"s","stock":"NOCK5"},{"price":40,"volume":10,"init":"s","stock":"NOCK5"}]
[{"price":17,"volume":85,"init":"s","stock":"NOCK3"}]
[{"price":37,"volume":99,"init":"b","stock":"NOCK5"}]
[{"price":57,"volume":82,"init":"s","stock":"NOCK4"}]
[{"price":17,"volume":108,"init":"s","stock":"NOCK3"}]
[{"price":48,"volume":86,"init":"b","stock":"NOCK2"}]
[{"price":17,"volume":54,"init":"s","stock":"NOCK3"},{"price":16,"volume":60,"init":"s","stock":"NOCK3"}]
[{"price":49,"volume":103,"init":"s","stock":"NOCK2"}]
[{"price":57,"volume":112,"init":"s","stock":"NOCK4"}]
```

Figure 5.5. The Chrome console prints stock prices

Nice work! You now have built a real-time trading exchange in Node.js with the data streaming to multiple connected clients in real time. For those of you without access to a console, don't worry; you're not missing out on anything. This is simply an intermediate step to provide some evidence that data is finding its way into the browser. In Chapter 6, we'll move from the console directly to the page, where you'll see ample evidence that data is being received by the user.

Forms Begone

To date, we have been handling user input either via forms or the more advanced Ajax. Socket.IO introduces some interesting possibilities. Why, you may ask, would we want to use Socket.IO for a purpose that is already served by existing technology? There are several reasons.

First, it allows us to unclutter our routes. To date, we've been using routes as a glue to bind our front-end views to our back-end business logic. As applications become larger, the routing file inevitably becomes cluttered, no matter how well it's structured. Socket.IO enables us to bypass the routing table entirely, essentially allowing the front-end view to communicate directly with the business logic.

Second, Socket.IO uses a superior transport protocol. If available, it uses WebSocket, which incurs less overhead than XMLHttpRequest and has the added benefit of supporting bidirectional communication.

Third, your application is future-proofed. It never directly deals with a specific protocol such as WebSocket; instead, it only uses the Socket.IO API. This means that whenever the next latest and greatest technology comes along, your application will be able to capitalize by simply upgrading the Socket.IO library. In contrast,

Ajax is tied to a specific implementation, namely XMLHttpRequest. To switch this across to another protocol would involve a nontrivial rewrite of code.

 Socket.IO API Changes

While we state that all you'll need to do is upgrade your Socket.IO library to keep up to date with the latest technology, this only holds true as long as Socket.IO maintains its existing underlying API or architecture. Within the Node.js community, convention dictates that version numbers below 1.0 are considered to be betas, which means that end users should be prepared for API changes between versions. After 1.0, the product is generally more stable, and future releases tend to be backward-compatible.

As of the time of writing, Socket.IO is currently at v0.9.x. The release of v1.0 will mean that you as an end user will have considerably less concern over backward-compatibility compared to some of the less mature packages currently in use within the Node.js ecosystem.

We will now implement a simple form that enables users to update their email addresses. First, let's modify our **portfolio.ejs** template to include an extra tab with account details:

chapter05/views/portfolio.ejs (excerpt)

```
<script src="/js/trades.js"></script>
<script src="/js/account.js"></script>
⋮
<li><a href="#tab3" data-toggle="tab" id="chat-tab">Chat</a></li>
<li><a href="#tab4" data-toggle="tab">My Account</a></li>
⋮
  <p><span class="label label-inverse chat-widget" id="online">
    Online:</span><div id="users"></div></p>
</div>
<div class="tab-pane" id="tab4">
  <p><input type="text" class="input-xlarge span8" id="email"></p>
  <p><button type="submit" class="btn btn-primary"
    id="update-account">Update</button></p>
</div>
```

There's nothing new to learn here; it's very similar to code we've previously written. On the back end, we have to make a few additions. First, we modify **db.js**, adding a function that allows us to modify user data:

chapter05/lib/db.js *(excerpt)*

```
push: function(name, id, updateQuery, callback) {
  ⋮
},
updateById: function(name, id, updateQuery, callback) {
  db.collection(name).update({_id: id}, {$set: updateQuery}
    , {safe:true}, callback);
}
```

This is very similar to our push function, except instead of using the $push modifier, we use $set to update the specified fields in our database. To use this function, we link it to a function in **nocklib.js** as follows:

chapter05/lib/nocklib.js *(excerpt)*

```
sendTrades: function(trades) {
  ⋮
},

updateEmail: function(id, email, callback) {
  db.updateById('users', new ObjectID(id)
    , {email: email}, callback);
}
```

We update user emails by calling our generic update function with a specific collection, being users, and a specific query, being {email: email}. Lastly, we modify createSocket to handle the message from the client:

chapter05/lib/nocklib.js *(excerpt)*

```
socket.on('joined', function (data) {
  ⋮
});
socket.on('updateAccount', function (data) {
  module.exports.updateEmail(socket.handshake.session._id,
    data.email, function(err, numUpdates) {
    // Send a response back to the client here
  });
});
```

The last job to do is to create **/public/js/account.js** as follows:

```
$(document).ready(function() {
  $('#update-account').click(function() {
    socket.emit('updateAccount', {email: $('#email').val()});
  });
});
```

To verify that we're actually storing the email address, we can modify the portfolio function in **nockroutes.js** to pass the email address to the template:

```
res.render('portfolio', {portfolio: portfolio, prices: prices
  , email: user.email});
```

We can then touch up **portfolio.ejs** to display the user's email address:

```
<input type="text" class="input-xlarge span8" id="email"
  value="<%=email%>"></p>
```

Now if you update your email address and refresh the page, the text field will correctly show the new email address. Let's finish the chapter with a bit of a flourish. We'll display a confirmation message letting users know that their email address has been updated correctly. On the server side, we merely add a single line of code to **nocklib.js** to indicate success to the client:

```
module.exports.updateEmail(socket.handshake.session._id, data.email
  , function(err, numUpdates) {
    socket.emit('updateSuccess', {});
});
```

In **/public/js/account.js**, we can display the alert by appending the following:

chapter05/public/js/account.js

```
socket.on('updateSuccess', function (data) {
  var html = "<div class='alert alert-success'>
    <i class='icon-ok'></i> Email updated!</div>";
  $(html).hide()
    .appendTo('h3').fadeIn("fast").delay("2000").fadeOut("fast");
});
```

Here we process the message by using a Bootstrap alert, which we fade in, then out. Now when you update your email address, you should see what's in Figure 5.6.

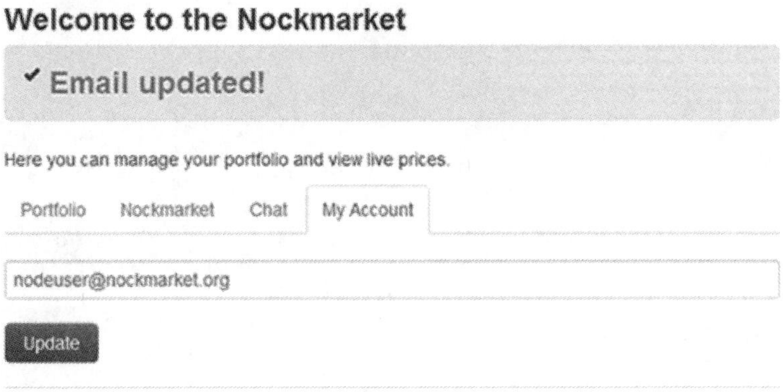

Welcome to the Nockmarket

✔ **Email updated!**

Here you can manage your portfolio and view live prices.

Portfolio   Nockmarket   Chat   My Account

nodeuser@nockmarket.org

Update

Figure 5.6. Your email address is now up to date!

The message should fade out after a few seconds. Time to pat yourself on the back, as you have achieved quite a lot in this chapter. Using Socket.IO, you have built a real-time chat system, transmitted real-time trades to the browser, and built a fast alternative to the traditional Ajax/forms solution.

Summary

In this chapter, we have learned the following:

- authentication with Socket.IO
- how to create a basic real-time chat application
- detecting and displaying connecting and disconnecting users
- updating our simulated stock market to incorporate an arbitrary number of stocks
- sending real-time trading data through Socket.IO
- using Socket.IO as a replacement for forms and AJAX

6

Backbone

> "Chaos was the law of nature; order was the dream of man."
>
> —Henry B. Adams

Software engineering is about managing complexity; it's a theme to which we keep returning, but it cannot be emphasized enough. So, far we have looked at a number of ways to manage complexity on the server side; however, we've yet to discuss complexity management on the client side. To date, we have been managing client-side code by annotating HTML tags and then manipulating them through jQuery. While this works for smaller projects, the ability to manage complexity rapidly breaks down as the size of the code base increases.

There are many client-side frameworks built for managing this type of problem. In this chapter, we'll look at one of the more popular ones, Backbone.js.[1] Backbone loosely follows the **MVC** model in which an application is split into models, views, and controllers. We'll look at how Backbone can be combined with Node.js to present a real-time graphical user interface to the end user showing orders and trades. While

---

[1] http://backbonejs.org/

the initial learning curve is a little steep, the end result is an elegant solution to managing client-side code that will scale to a larger code base as needed.

Models, Views, Controllers, and Backbone.js

A comprehensive treatment of MVC and Backbone is a book in and of itself. For the uninitiated, there's no need to fret; this chapter's designed to be followed by those new to both MVC and Backbone. However, for those who wish to explore them in further detail, some recommended resources are listed here:

http://net.tutsplus.com/tutorials/other/mvc-for-noobs/
A brief introduction to MVC, it is written with PHP as the target language. This is advantageous insofar as the reader can concentrate purely on the architectural aspects without becoming mired in language considerations.

http://backbonejs.org/#FAQ-mvc
This snippet from the official Backbone documentation explains how traditional MVC fits in with the Backbone approach.

https://github.com/addyosmani/backbone-fundamentals
An open-source book dedicated to explaining Backbone in considerable detail.

https://github.com/documentcloud/backbone/wiki/Tutorials%2C-blog-posts-and-example-sites
A comprehensive repository of Backbone examples and tutorials.

Sneak Preview

There are quite a few concepts to cover before we reach the big payoff. Let's build a quick mockup of the final product that we're working towards, as it will provide a handy roadmap to guide us. We'll start with a simple Bootstrap mockup.

The code is plain HTML and can be retrieved at https://gist.github.com/3949965. Copy the code and paste it into **portfolio.ejs** as follows:

chapter06/views/portfolio.ejs *(excerpt)*

```
<div class="tab-pane" id="tab2">
  <!-- Paste code here -->
</div>
```

Your **Nockmarket** tab should now resemble Figure 6.1.

Welcome to the Nockmarket

Here you can manage your portfolio and view live prices.

Portfolio	Nockmarket	Chat	My Account

Stock	BID5	BID4	BID3	BID2	BID1	Trade	ASK1	ASK2	ASK3	ASK4	ASK5
NOCK1	20.4	20.9	21.2	22.0	22.5	23.2	23.5	23.9	24.4	24.9	25.1
	2004	1932	429	6244	397	142	4286	1972	942	896	325

Figure 6.1. **Nockmarket** tab showing prices

Client Filtering

We will implement a filter that allows the user to filter their portfolio based on the code of a particular stock. There are several approaches to this, the least efficient being a traditional form submission. This involves an entire page refresh including portions of the page that we know will stay the same.

A better approach is to use Ajax, as it will only change that part of the page that involves new data. This will be quicker than a full page refresh, but there is still a call to the server, which may cause a sluggish experience depending on the connection between the user and your site.

It's possible to construct an ad hoc approach to solving the client-side problem by combining jQuery with HTML tag annotations. Backbone is a lightweight framework that will enforce a consistent approach all the way through. Using a framework like this is preferred because it will promote code readability and maintainability.

Our first task is to change the way that the initial stock portfolio is transmitted from the server to the client. At the moment, the user makes a request, the data is assembled on the server, and it is then fed into a template and rendered to the user.

The Backbone approach is as follows. As before, the user makes a request. Backbone then makes a request to a server-side API. The data is placed into a model on the client side. Subsequent changes are made to the model and bindings specify how these changes should be reflected in the user interface. Let's proceed with a concrete example to help illustrate the concept. Modify **portfolio.ejs** as follows:

chapter06/views/portfolio.ejs *(excerpt)*

```
<script type="text/javascript" src="http://twitter.github.com/
➥bootstrap/assets/js/bootstrap-tab.js"></script>
<script src="http://documentcloud.github.com/
➥underscore/underscore-min.js"></script>
<script src="http://backbonejs.org/backbone-min.js"></script>
```

Backbone relies on another small library called Underscore.[2] Both should be placed just before we begin our own JavaScript. Now modify **public/js/portfolio.js** as follows:

chapter06/public/js/portfolio.js *(excerpt)*

```
    $('.stock-list').append('<tr><td>' + $('#stock').val()
       + '</td><td>' + price + '</td></tr>');
  });
});

var PortfolioView = Backbone.View.extend({
  initialize: function() {
    this.render();
  },
  render: function() {
    $('.stock-list').html('<tr><td>1</td><td>2</td></tr>');
  }
});
new PortfolioView();
});
```

This is one of the simplest Backbone applications possible. There is one function, initialize, which is called at the start. This then calls the render function, which sets the contents of our table. If you now go to the **Portfolio** tab, you'll see that our data has been replaced with some dummy data.

Let's now modify this example to return the real data. Most of the back end has already been done. We just have to make one small adjustment to **nockroutes.js**:

---

[2] http://underscorejs.org/

chapter06/routes/nockroutes.js *(excerpt)*

```
nocklib.getStockPrices(portfolio, function(err, prices) {
  if (req.xhr) {
    var data = [];
    for (var i = 0; i < portfolio.length; i++) {
      data.push({stock: portfolio[i], price: prices[i]});
    }
    res.json(data);
  } else {
    res.render('portfolio', {portfolio: portfolio, prices: prices
      , email: user.email});
  }
});
```

We use `req.xhr` to detect Ajax requests. In the event of Ajax, we construct an array
of data consisting of stock names and prices. We send back raw JSON instead of
HTML, as can be seen by the call to `res.json`. Note that we still need to use Ajax
for the initial data load. Information still has to get from the server to the client!
The advantage of the Backbone.js is that subsequent changes can be performed on
the client entirely, as long as no new information is required.

A Backbone Model

Let's see how Backbone deals with models. First of all, we can define a basic model
and collection in **public/js/portfolio.js**:

chapter06/public/js/portfolio.js *(excerpt)*

```
});

var PortfolioModel = Backbone.Model.extend({
});

var PortfolioCollection = Backbone.Collection.extend({
  model: PortfolioModel,
  url: '/portfolio'
});

var PortfolioView = Backbone.View.extend({
```

Here we define a basic model by extending the stock Backbone model. We then
define a collection by specifying our model and a URL. `url` defines the path to our

JSON API. We can then use our newly defined components by modifying the `initialize` function:

chapter06/public/js/portfolio.js *(excerpt)*

```
initialize: function() {
  window.portfolioCollection = new PortfolioCollection();
  window.portfolioCollection.fetch({
    success: function() {
      console.log(window.portfolioCollection.toJSON());
    },
    error: function() {
      console.log('Error fetching data for portfolio');
    }
  });
},
render: function() {
```

Here we initialize the collection and use the built-in `fetch` to retrieve the data from the API. If there's an error, we print an error message. When successful, we log the JSON data for now. There is still a bit of console clutter from Chapter 5, so comment out the logging in **public/js/trades.js** as follows:

chapter06/public/js/trades.js *(excerpt)*

```
socket.on('trade', function (data) {
  //console.log(data);
});
```

Now when you restart the application, you should have a similar view to Figure 6.2 printed to your console:

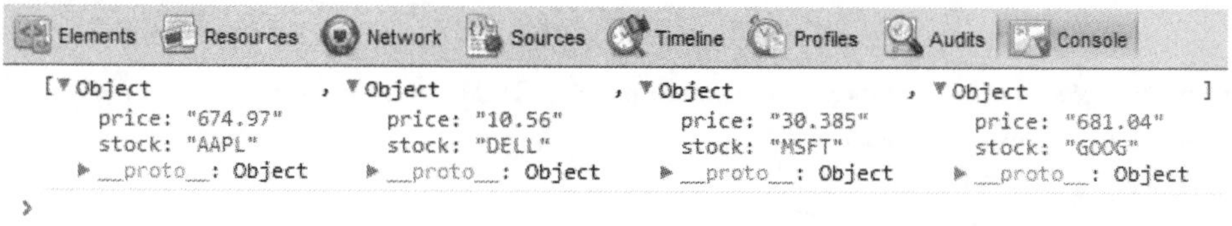

Figure 6.2. Backbone console output

No Console, No Problems

If you lack access to the console of your browser, don't worry. This is simply an intermediate step; very soon, we'll have all the data back in the browser.

From Model to View

How is the data from the model rendered into a view? We'll look at that now. First, let's remove the template code that prints out the list of stocks. This is the "old way" of rendering, and we'll be replacing it with the Backbone approach. Modify **portfolio.ejs** as follows:

chapter06/views/portfolio.ejs *(excerpt)*

```
<tbody class="stock-list">
  <!-- delete everything here -->
</tbody>
```

Now let's modify the `success` function in **portfolio.js** to call `render`, instead of printing a message to the console:

chapter06/public/js/portfolio.js *(excerpt)*

```
var self = this;
window.portfolioCollection.fetch({
success: function() {
  self.render();
},
```

To those with limited JavaScript experience, `self = this` might seem confusing code. We do this because in JavaScript, the keyword `this` is contextual. A full explanation involves quite a lot of detail.[3] Suffice to say, we store the value of the `PortfolioView` instance in a variable called `self` so that we can be sure about its value, no matter where it needs to be used. We then modify `render` as follows:

---

[3] http://www.quirksmode.org/js/this.html

```
render: function() {
  for (var i=0; i<window.portfolioCollection.models.length; i++) {
    var data = window.portfolioCollection.models[i];
    var rowView = new RowView({model: data});
    $('.stock-list').append(rowView.render().el);
  }
}
}
```

Here we begin by iterating over all the models. We then feed each model into a RowView, which we're about to define. We want a separate view for individual table rows because it allows us maximum granularity when it comes to controlling the presentation. We then define RowView as follows:

```
});

var RowView = Backbone.View.extend({
  tagName: 'tr',
  render: function() {
    var template =
      _.template("<td><%=stock%></td><td><%=price%></td>");
    $(this.el).html(template(this.model.toJSON()));
    return this;
  }
});
new PortfolioView();
```

The el and tagName variables may initially be slightly confusing. The official documentation describes them thus:[4]

> "All views have a DOM element at all times (the el property), whether they've already been inserted into the page or not. In this fashion, views can be rendered at any time, and inserted into the DOM all at once, in order to get high-performance UI rendering with as few reflows and repaints as possible. this.el is created from the

---

[4] http://backbonejs.org/#View-el

view's `tagName`, `className`, `id` and `attributes` properties, if specified. If not, `el` is an empty `div`."

—Backbone.js

In this particular case, `el` is the `tr` tag. When we call `render`, the actual HTML content appears between `<tr></tr>` tags. We use Backbone's sister library, Underscore, to construct a template:

```
var template = _.template(...);
```

Then we convert the model into JSON:

```
this.model.toJSON()
```

… and feed it into the template, which will return plain HTML. Once we have the HTML, we can append each row to the table body. Now if you refresh the page, the original list of stocks and prices should once again appear on the screen. That's a lot of work just to return to where we were before. However, we will now add client-side filtering where the benefit of Backbone will become more apparent.

Client Filters

To start, let's modify **portfolio.ejs** and add a Bootstrap widget:

chapter06/views/portfolio.ejs (excerpt)

```
<button id="add-stock" class="btn">Add Stock</button><hr />
<input id="filter" type="text" class="input-medium search-query"
  name="filter">
<button class="add-filter btn">Filter</button>
```

You should now have a **Filter** button just below your **Add Stock** button. First, we'll change our model as follows:

chapter06/public/js/portfolio.js (excerpt)

```
var PortfolioModel = Backbone.Model.extend({
  defaults: {
    visible: true
  },
  setVisible: function(visible) {
```

```
        this.set({visible: visible});
    }
});
```

Other than stock code and price, we add a visibility property to our model, which will be used to control whether or not the data is visible on the screen. We then modify PortfolioView as follows:

chapter06/public/js/portfolio.js *(excerpt)*

```
var PortfolioView = Backbone.View.extend({
  el: 'body',
    events: {
      'click .add-filter': 'filter'
    },
    filter: function() {
      var filterString = $('#filter').val();
      var data = window.portfolioCollection.models;
      for (var i=0; i<data.length; i++) {
        if (data[i].toJSON().stock.toLowerCase()
          .indexOf(filterString.toLowerCase()) == -1) {
            data[i].setVisible(false);
        }
        else data[i].setVisible(true);
      }
    },
  initialize: function() {
```

We set el to the body tag, and then add a single event:

```
'click .add-filter': 'filter'
```

This means that when anybody clicks on an element with the class add-filter, our filter function will be triggered. In our filter function, we retrieve the search term and compare it to each of the stock codes by converting it to lower case and using JavaScript's built-in indexOf function. Critically, all we do at this point is modify the visibility property of the model using setVisible. No code is actually specified relating to the view. The view code is handled by RowView as follows:

```
                                    chapter06/public/js/portfolio.js (excerpt)
var RowView = Backbone.View.extend({
  tagName: 'tr',
  initialize: function() {
    _.bindAll(this, 'setVisibility');
    this.model.bind('change', this.setVisibility);
  },
  setVisibility: function() {
    if (!this.model.toJSON().visible) $(this.el).hide();
    else $(this.el).show();
  },
  render: function() {
```

This is the crux of the Backbone solution. In the `initialize` function, we bind a change in the model to the `setVisibility` function. In `setVisibility`, we can query properties and set the view accordingly. Here we query the `visible` property and use jQuery's `show` and `hide` to perform the relevant operation. Now when you enter a term for filtering, the stock list should be updated accordingly. Run your app and notice the clean separation between business logic, models, and views. This separation is what will keep your code base readable and maintainable.

Real-time Trades

Now it's time to reap the rewards of all the hard work we've put in so far. By the end of this section, you'll have real-time trades appearing in your browser.

We will break this down into two parts. In the first part, we'll initialize the models and load an initial data set when the client connects. A lot of the concepts here will be similar to what we've just done in implementing client filters. In the second part, we'll use our models and collections to update the data in real time.

We begin by declaring a variable in **nocklib.js** to store the most recent exchange data:

```
                                        chapter06/lib/nocklib.js (excerpt)
var online = [];
var lastExchangeData = {};
```

Now let's add a function to store the exchange data every time it changes:

chapter06/lib/nocklib.js *(excerpt)*

```
},

sendExchangeData: function(stock, exchangeData) {
  lastExchangeData[stock] = exchangeData;
  var current = transformStockData(stock, exchangeData);
  io.sockets.emit('exchangeData', current);
},

sendTrades: function(trades) {
```

The first task is to store the data. Then we transform it and send it to the client. Add the transformation function to the bottom of **nocklib.js** as follows:

chapter06/lib/nocklib.js *(excerpt)*

```
function transformStockData(stock, existingData) {
  var newData = {};
  newData.st = stock;
  if (existingData && existingData.trades
    && existingData.trades.length > 0) {
      newData.tp = existingData.trades[0].price;
      newData.tv = existingData.trades[0].volume;
  }
}
```

We transform the data because it would be inefficient to transmit the entire block of exchange data down the wire. Loading time is a precious commodity and the less data we transmit, the better the experience. In the previous code, we look for trades, and if they exist we truncate them down to **tp** for trade price and **tv** for trade volume. Following similar logic, we transform bids and asks as follows:

chapter06/lib/nocklib.js *(excerpt)*

```
  if (existingData && existingData.trades
    && existingData.trades.length > 0) {
      ⋮
  }
  var buyPrices = {};
  var askPrices = {};
  if (existingData && existingData.buys) {
    buyPrices = Object.keys(existingData.buys.volumes);
```

```
      for (var i=buyPrices.length - 5; i<buyPrices.length; i++) {
        var index = buyPrices.length - i;
        newData['b' + index + 'p'] = buyPrices[i];
        newData['b' + index + 'v'] = existingData
          .buys.volumes[buyPrices[i]];
      }
    }
    if (existingData && existingData.sells)    {
      askPrices = Object.keys(existingData.sells.volumes);
      for (var i=0; i<5; i++) {
        var index = i + 1;
        newData['a' + index + 'p'] = askPrices[i];
        newData['a' + index + 'v'] = existingData
          .sells.volumes[askPrices[i]];
      }
    }
    return newData;
}
```

Instead of transmitting the entire order book to the client, we simply take the orders to a depth of five, since this is what will be displayed on the client. We then assign codes such as b1p for the first bid price, b1v for the first bid volume, and so on. Lastly, we add some fillers for nonexistent values:

chapter06/lib/nocklib.js *(excerpt)*

```
}
for (var i = 1; i <= 5; i++) {
  if (!newData['b' + i + 'p']) {
    newData['b' + i + 'p'] = 0;
    newData['b' + i + 'v'] = 0;
  }
  if (!newData['a' + i + 'p']) {
    newData['a' + i + 'p'] = 0;
    newData['a' + i + 'v'] = 0;
  }
  if (!newData['tv']) {
    newData['tv'] = 0;
  }
  if (!newData['tp']) {
    newData['tp'] = 0;
  }
}
return newData;
```

Efficiency

The aforementioned data schema could be improved further. For example, we could just send arrays of data down to the client, and have more business and parsing logic on the client. My preference is to have business logic controlled by the server. I lean towards having "dumb" clients that simply print information provided by the server, but you are free to play with this balance depending on the particular business needs of your project.

Now when the client makes the initial request, we can transmit the exchange data down in this more compact format:

chapter06/lib/nocklib.js (excerpt)

```
});
socket.on('requestData', function (data) {
  socket.emit('initExchangeData'
    , {exchangeData: transformExchangeData(lastExchangeData)});
});
socket.on('updateAccount', function (data) {
```

`'requestData'` is a message transmitted by the client that we'll implement later in the chapter. We'll need a helper function to iterate through every stock in the exchange and truncate the data before sending it to the client:

chapter06/lib/nocklib.js (excerpt)

```
function transformExchangeData(data) {
  var transformed = [];
  for (var stock in data) {
    var existingData = data[stock];
    var newData = transformStockData(stock, existingData);
    transformed.push(newData);
  }
  return transformed;
}

function transformStockData(stock, existingData) {
```

Finally, let's modify **nockmarket.js** so that it sends all the exchange data:

```
});
nocklib.sendExchangeData(stocks[index], exchangeData);
db.insert('transactions', trades, function(err, trades) {
```

We used trades previously for simplification. It would have been too confusing to print everything in the console. Now that we can present it graphically, this is no longer an issue. It's time to construct the models and collections on the client.

Loading Trade Data

Although the business problem is different, a lot of the concepts learned when building a client-side filter apply to the problem of real-time trades. Still, there are some differences that need to be addressed. First, the template is more complicated so it would be awkward to simply store it in a string. Create a new folder called **public/templates**, and then generate **trade-table.ejs** by pasting the code from https://gist.github.com/3949967.

Alternative Client-side Templates

Another common way to embed client-side templates is to put your template inside your main HTML page within `<script type = "text/template"></script>` tags. In this case, we have a peculiar scenario because we're using the same templating syntax on both the server and the client. This presents an interesting challenge, because the server will throw an error as it tries to interpret the client-side tags. There are various workarounds you could use, such as changing template settings to using an alternative syntax. I will leave this for the curious reader to explore as an exercise.

It's a slightly unwieldy block of code that would have maintenance issues were we to embed it inside a JavaScript file. A dedicated template allows separation of presentation and business logic. If the size of the code appears intimidating, broken down it's just a series of HTML `td` tags with some `ids` thrown in. It's a slightly more elaborate version of the mockup we wrote in the section called "Sneak Preview". To complete the HTML side, add a small annotation in **portfolio.ejs** as follows:

chapter06/views/portfolio.ejs *(excerpt)*

```
    </thead>
    <tbody class="stock-data">
    </tbody>
  </table>
</div>
<div class="tab-pane" id="tab3">
```

Now let's make the client side display the data. There's very little in **trades.js**, so let's start it afresh and retrieve the template as follows:

chapter06/public/js/trades.js *(excerpt)*

```
$(document).ready(function() {
  $.get('/templates/trade-table.ejs', function(storedTemplate) {
  });
});
```

We use jQuery's get function to retrieve the template. As before, we set up some basic stubs for the model and collection, and send an initial 'requestData' message to the server so that the initial data can be sent:

chapter06/public/js/trades.js *(excerpt)*

```
$.get('/templates/trade-table.ejs', function(storedTemplate) {
  socket.emit('requestData', {});
  var StockModel = Backbone.Model.extend({
  });
  var StockCollection = Backbone.Collection.extend({
    model: StockModel
  });
});
```

Now we handle the initial data transmission from the server:

chapter06/public/js/trades.js *(excerpt)*

```
var StockCollection = Backbone.Collection.extend({
  model: StockModel
});
socket.on('initExchangeData', function (data) {
  window.stockCollection = new StockCollection();
```

```
    for (var stock in data.exchangeData) {
      var stockModel = new StockModel(data.exchangeData[stock]);
      stockModel.set({id: data.exchangeData[stock].st});
      window.stockCollection.push(stockModel);
    }
    new StockView();
});
```

This is similar to loading the user's portfolio. The main difference is we set the id
field to the stock code for easy reference down the line:

```
stockModel.set({id: data.exchangeData[stock].st});
```

Then we define the overall view:

chapter06/public/js/trades.js *(excerpt)*

```
var StockCollection = Backbone.Collection.extend({
  model: StockModel
});
var StockView = Backbone.View.extend({
  initialize: function() {
    var self = this;
    self.render();
  },
  render: function() {
    for (var i=0; i<window.stockCollection.models.length; i++) {
      var data = window.stockCollection.models[i];
      var rowView = new StockRowView({model: data});
      $('.stock-data').append(rowView.render().el);
    }
  }
});
```

As before, we use initialize to call the render function. Inside render, we iterate
through all the models and then render each row individually with a separate view.
The individual row view is defined as follows:

chapter06/public/js/trades.js *(excerpt)*

```
var StockRowView = Backbone.View.extend({
  tagName: 'tr',
  render: function() {
```

```
    var template = _.template(storedTemplate);
    var htmlString = template(this.model.toJSON());
    $(this.el).html(htmlString);
    return this;
  }
});
socket.on('initExchangeData', function (data) {
```

Instead of using a string as the template, we use the stored template that we have retrieved through jQuery's get function. Then we render the template and return it. Now when you run the application and give it a minute for some trades to occur, you should see some static data similar to Figure 6.3.

Welcome to the Nockmarket

Here you can manage your portfolio and view live prices.

Portfolio   Nockmarket   Chat   My Account

Stock	BID5	BID4	BID3	BID2	BID1	Trade	ASK1	ASK2	ASK3	ASK4	ASK5
NOCK1	20.4 / 2004	20.9 / 1932	21.2 / 429	22.0 / 6244	22.5 / 397	23.2 / 142	23.5 / 4286	23.9 / 1972	24.4 / 942	24.9 / 896	25.1 / 325
NOCK3	42 / 636	43 / 1466	44 / 2470	45 / 2091	48 / 212	51 / 89	51 / 20	52 / 2156	53 / 2011	54 / 895	55 / 706
NOCK5	32 / 384	33 / 1372	34 / 3012	35 / 602	37 / 94	38 / 100	39 / 487	40 / 301	41 / 683	42 / 299	43 / 1455
NOCK4	21 / 644	22 / 1650	23 / 1737	24 / 1652	25 / 100	25 / 97	27 / 84	28 / 515	29 / 750	30 / 793	31 / 584
NOCK1	11 / 591	12 / 1889	13 / 1171	14 / 1164	15 / 292	21 / 104	21 / 500	22 / 1435	23 / 806	24 / 691	25 / 103
NOCK2	36 / 1013	37 / 1535	38 / 1005	39 / 200	40 / 82	41 / 86	43 / 99	44 / 2270	45 / 1543	46 / 1320	47 / 376

Figure 6.3. A static market

So now it is beginning to resemble a real stock board. At the moment, the data is completely static, but it's now time for the big payoff: real-time trades.

Backbone Patterns

Even with just the two examples so far, you can see that patterns are beginning to emerge. Although it may seem we're writing a lot of boilerplate code, it's my intention to take you through everything from first principles so that you understand what is happening behind the scenes.

node-toolbox[5] has many Backbone.js related packages. Some of them can take a mongodb update and run the change automatically all the way through to a front-end Backbone.js model. Feel free to explore the packages at your leisure, safe in the knowledge that you have the ability to replicate that same functionality from scratch should you so choose.

Your Very Own Market

There are only a few more steps to complete. First of all, we just wish to process updates after the initial load of the data has taken place. Add a variable in **trades.js** to track this as follows:

chapter06/public/js/trades.js *(excerpt)*

```
var loaded = false;
socket.emit('requestData', {});
```

We set this variable to `true` once we've processed the initial data:

chapter06/public/js/trades.js *(excerpt)*

```
loaded = true;
new StockView();
```

When the data is updated, all we need to do is retrieve the model and subsequently call an update function:

chapter06/public/js/trades.js *(excerpt)*

```
socket.on('exchangeData', function (deltas) {
  if (loaded) {
    var model = window.stockCollection.get(deltas.st);
```

---

[5] http://toolbox.no.de/

```
      model.updatePrices(deltas);
  }
});
socket.on('initExchangeData', function (data) {
```

Earlier, we set the id to the stock code, so we can now use the built-in get function to retrieve the model from the collection. We then call our own updatePrices function, which we can define as follows:

chapter06/public/js/trades.js *(excerpt)*

```
var StockModel = Backbone.Model.extend({
  updatePrices: function(deltas) {
    this.set({deltas: deltas});
  }
});
```

In updatePrices, we simply have to call the set function. Then in the row view, we bind a data change to a function that can update the view:

chapter06/public/js/trades.js *(excerpt)*

```
tagName: 'tr',
initialize: function() {
  _.bindAll(this, 'setPrices');
  this.model.bind('change', this.setPrices);
},
```

The last link in the chain is the setPrices function. It is here that the user interface is manipulated. For setPrices, all we'll do for now is iterate through the prices and set the HTML if we have a price greater than zero:

chapter06/public/js/trades.js *(excerpt)*

```
render: function() {
  var template = _.template(storedTemplate);
  var htmlString = template(this.model.toJSON());
  $(this.el).html(htmlString);
   return this;
},
setPrices: function() {
  var color = "#82FA58";
```

```
  var prices = this.model.toJSON().deltas;
  for (var attr in prices) {
    var value = prices[attr];
    if (value > 0) {
      if (attr == 'tp') {
        $('#' + prices.st + 'trade-cell')
          .css("backgroundColor", color);
        $('#' + prices.st + 'trade-cell')
          .animate({backgroundColor: "white"}, 1000);
      }
      $('#' + prices.st + attr).html(value);
    }
  }
}
```

You should now have live trades coming into your browser. Now to tidy up. First, our mock data row is still there, so delete that in **views/portfolio.ejs**:

chapter06/views/portfolio.ejs *(excerpt)*

```
    <tr>
      <!-- delete everything here -->
    </tr>
  </thead>
  <tbody class="stock-data">
  </tbody>
</table>
```

Lastly, the interface is a little "jumpy" because the boxes keep changing in size as the numbers update. We can fix this by making the boxes a fixed width. Create **public/stylesheets/nockmarket.css** as follows:

chapter06/public/stylesheets/nockmarket.css

```
.trade-button {
  width: 24px;
}
```

Then add to **portfolio.ejs** as follows:

```
<link href="/stylesheets/nockmarket.css" rel="stylesheet">
<script src="http://twitter.github.com/bootstrap/assets/js/
➥google-code-prettify/prettify.js"></script>
```

Now all the boxes should be of a fixed width, making the interface smoother. Congratulations, you should now have real-time trades updating in your browser! It was a lot of work, but it all paid off in the end. There is still some polishing to do to make the interface even better, but we'll leave that to the next chapter.

Summary

In this chapter, we have learned about:

- using Backbone for separation of functionality on the client side
- the basics of models, collections, and views in Backbone
- retrieving data from a server-side JSON API and insert it into a Backbone model
- implementing a pure client-side filter
- streaming real-time trades into a browser

Chapter **7**

Production

> "Art is never finished, only abandoned."
>
> —Leonardo da Vinci

This chapter is all about production. Once you've built your shiny new application, you need to know how to transfer it from your local machine to display it to the rest of the world. Fortunately, there are a multitude of hosting options out there, many of which are free. In this chapter, we will cover deploying with a specific provider, Heroku.

We will cover some of the differences between a production deployment and a local development environment. Many of these production techniques will apply regardless of the environment you end up choosing. So if you decide to go with a provider other than Heroku, the knowledge acquired in this chapter will be applicable to your final choice. By the end of the book, you will have a live deployment.

Development versus Production

Express.js supports both development and production settings. One of the differences between the two is in the way errors are handled. In development, it's handy to have a comprehensive stack trace displayed in the browser when an error occurs. In production, you almost never want to display detailed error information. For example, for security reasons you may wish to hide how your systems operate.

Add the following to **nockmarket.js**:

```
app.configure('development', function () {
  app.use(express.errorHandler(
    {dumpExceptions:true, showStack:true }));
});
app.configure('production', function () {
  app.use(express.errorHandler());
});
app.set('view options', {
```

We've configured development and production settings. The development settings display verbose error information. To test this, modify **nockroutes.js** to throw an error:

```
getIndex: function(req, res) {
  throw new Error('dummy error');
  res.render('index');
},
```

If you go to http://localhost:3000, you should receive an error message similar to:

```
Error: dummy error
    at module.exports.getIndex (...)
    ⋮
    at Object.oncomplete (fs.js:297:15)
```

Let's now try starting in production mode to see what happens. There are several ways to do this. For a one-off run, you can execute the following command:

```
NODE_ENV=production node nockmarket.js
```

While this will run the application in production mode, subsequent runs will be in normal development mode. For a more permanent option, we can set the NODE_ENV environment variable as follows:

```
export NODE_ENV=production
```

This will ensure that the application is run in production mode irrespective of how many times the application is restarted. The environment variable will be retained for the duration of your shell session. If you wish to keep the settings across reboots, there are a number of references that will help you with the correct configuration.[1]

Now that you are running in production mode, when you visit the home page, you should receive the much more cryptic ...

```
Internal Server Error
```

Other tasks that might require different development and production settings include logging, email, and ecommerce. The exact development and production settings will depend on the business case; however, you now understand the basic mechanism behind controlling the environment. Remember to delete the dummy error.

There is nothing magical about "development" and "production." They are just arbitrary strings; you could use others such as "staging" and "test." In fact, you could use a single configuration for multiple environments as follows:

```
app.configure('production', 'test', function(){ … });
```

404 Not Found

Another issue that requires our attention is the dreaded HTTP 404 Not Found error message. If you visit a page that doesn't exist, such as http://localhost:3000/blah, you'll receive the following message:

```
Cannot GET /blah
```

To offer a more friendly missive to our users, add this to the bottom of **nockmarket.js**:

---

[1] http://www.cyberciti.biz/faq/set-environment-variable-linux/

```
                                          chapter07/nockmarket.js (excerpt)
app.use(function(req, res){
  res.render('404');
});
```

Essentially, this provides a catchall, handling any request not processed by prior routes. Now create **views/404.ejs** as follows:

```
                                         chapter07/views/404.ejs (excerpt)
<!DOCTYPE html>
<html lang="en">
<head>
  <meta charset="utf-8">
  <title>404</title>
  <meta name="viewport"
    content="width=device-width, initial-scale=1.0">
  <link href="http://twitter.github.com/bootstrap/assets/css/
➥bootstrap.css" rel="stylesheet">
  <link href="http://spbooks.github.com/nodejs1/docs.css"
    rel="stylesheet">
</head>
<body>
<div class="container">
  <div class="marketing"><h1>Whoops</h1>
    <p class="marketing-byline">
      The page you are looking for cannot be found :(</p>
  </div>
</div>
</body>
</html>
```

Now when the user visits a nonexistent page, they'll receive a custom error message, the layout and content of which can be modified as desired.

Hosting Options

When it comes to hosting your application, there are several options available—each with its own advantages and disadvantages. The option that gives the most control is the dedicated server. Another possibility is Infrastructure as a Service (IaaS), with the most popular choice being Amazon's EC2. This option offers a number of conveniences over a dedicated server. The option we'll be using is Platform as a Service

(PaaS). This method offers the highest level of abstraction. A platform provider will handle your Node.js installation, as well as maintenance and upgrades, which allows you to devote full attention to your core competency of writing software.

Although an IaaS platform such as EC2 allows a systems administrator to easily bring new machines online, the actual setup and deployment of these machines can require a lot of scripting. Using a platform provider such as Heroku, scaling can sometimes be as easy as changing a configuration setting, with no need to reinstall either Node.js or your web application.

The cost of all this convenience is the loss of control. Often, you'll be without administrative access, and the level of abstraction is such that often you'll not even be dealing with a server. Instead, you interface with a platform through a custom-written set of tools. Your application will have to conform to the rules of the provider, and sometimes this can be inconvenient. For example, Heroku has an ephemeral file system, which means that any written files are discarded upon restarting.[2] Depending on the changes that are required, provider-specific code may also reduce the portability of your application.

Run It Forever

For those choosing to deploy on either a dedicated server or EC2, it's worth briefly visiting a more robust option than the humble `node nockmarket`. Perhaps by now you've realized that the stock standard way of running Node.js is a little unstable. An exception has the potential to cause the entire application to crash. In Real-world Development, I recommended node-supervisor as a mechanism for facilitating automatic restarts upon file change. This has the added side benefit of automatically restarting your application upon any crash. Unfortunately, this is unsuitable for production because behind the scenes, there is some fairly intensive file monitoring taking place that can cause unnecessary overhead.

Instead, I recommend a package called "forever," installed in the standard way:

```
sudo npm install -g forever
```

Starting your application is now as simple as:

---

[2] https://devcenter.heroku.com/articles/dynos#ephemeral-filesystem

```
forever start nockmarket.js
```

Aside from `start`, other common options include `stop` and `restart` (you can type `forever` at the prompt to see the full list). Now, for fairly minimal overhead you have a facility that will continually restart your application anytime there's an exit.

Let's move on to some of the basics behind deployment.

Version Control

Version control is a mechanism for controlling software changes. It is good practice to be using a version control system and absolutely mandatory if using Heroku. A number of popular version control systems exist, with the Node.js community very tightly intertwined with Git. Almost every single package is hosted on GitHub, an online provider of Git hosting services.

 An Introduction to Git

Git is a distributed version control system written by Linus Torvalds, the original developer of Linux. "Distributed" refers to the fact that you clone an entire repository, with the ability to make purely local changes before syncing to the main server. Every user has an entire backup of the full source code. Git also supports the concept of branching, which allows a developer to create branches for experimentation and new features. Other features are documented at the official site.[3]

We will cover Ubuntu. While development can take place on Mac OS X, Windows, or Linux, a production deployment is invariably done on some flavor of Linux, with Ubuntu being one of the more popular deployment options. Installation instructions for other platforms are available from the official website.[4]

Type the following at the command prompt:

```
sudo apt-get install git-core
```

[3] http://git-scm.com/about
[4] http://git-scm.com/

That's all that's needed for Git installation. Before versioning our software, create the file **.gitignore** at the top level so that we can specify what files and directories will be omitted. For now, it should contain a single line: `node_modules`.

There is no point checking in the modules directory. Heroku will automatically pull modules from the official repository whenever new code is checked in. Next, we create our Git repository as follows:

```
git init
```

Then we add files and directories:

```
git add .
```

This will add all files, directories, and subdirectories except for those specified in the ignore file. Now we can commit our files into a local repository with an initial message for documentation purposes:

```
git commit -m "Initial check in"
```

The above process creates a local repository. Each check-in is associated with a unique identifier. This allows us to revert to an arbitrary revision. Conceptually, we need to push this local repository to Heroku next. This process, along with a brief overview of Heroku, will be provided in the next section.

Heroku

Heroku is a polyglot Platform as a Service (PaaS) provider. **Polyglot** means that it supports several languages. Originally conceived as a host for Ruby, it now supports Java, Node.js, Scala, and Clojure. Platform as a Service is a model whereby Heroku provides the network and servers as well as the Node.js-related infrastructure. Heroku conveniently provides a free option, allowing us to comprehensively trial the offering before deciding whether to choose it as our final production host.

Because of Heroku's origins, both Ruby and its package manager, RubyGems, will be required before installing Heroku. If this is yet to be installed on your operating system, you can install both packages using the following command:

```
sudo apt-get install ruby-full rubygems
```

Nodejitsu

The Node.js ecosystem is constantly evolving and improving, and one of the newer hosting offerings comes from the team at Nodejitsu. A tutorial was not provided in this book because the product is currently still in beta. As such, it's not as battle-hardened as Heroku, and bugs and changes could potentially arise that would inconvenience you.

However, it is worth keeping an eye on this product as it matures. Because the offering is Node.js-specific, it requires fewer tweaks and customizations to your code base and environment. As an example, Nodejitsu has full support for Web-Sockets, and installation of its tools can take place through the node package manager (npm).

First, visit http://heroku.com and sign up for an account. Then execute the following command from your prompt:

```
wget -qO- https://toolbelt.heroku.com/install-ubuntu.sh | sh
```

This will install the Heroku toolbelt. Instructions for other operating systems are available at the official site.[5]

The toolbelt is controlled from the command line. You can log in to Heroku using:

```
heroku login
```

Configuration Tweaking

If you receive an error message about "command not found," you may need to set your path as per the https://devcenter.heroku.com/articles/cli-command-not-found instructions.

If you find that Heroku isn't installed in the specified EXECUTABLE_DIRECTORY, you can install it through gem as follows:

```
sudo gem install heroku
```

[5] https://toolbelt.herokuapp.com/

Enter your email and password; choose "Y" if you're asked to generate a public key.

 Public Keys

Heroku requires the use of public key encryption. It's easy to check whether you have a public key, and to generate one if you do not. The instructions are available at https://help.github.com/articles/generating-ssh-keys.

If you need to generate your public key manually, add it to Heroku:

```
heroku keys:add ~/.ssh/id_rsa.pub
```

Now we have to create a file called **Procfile** in the top level containing the following: `web: node nockmarket.js`.

web indicates that we are running a web application, which directly interfaces with the user. Heroku also supports worker processes designed to perform in the background. At this point, it's worth double-checking your **package.json** file. It should resemble the following:

chapter07/package.json *(excerpt)*

```
{
  "name": "nockmarket"
  , "version": "0.0.1"
  , "private": true
  , "engines": {
    "node": "0.8.8",
    "npm":  "1.1.49"
  }
  , "dependencies": {
    "cookie": "0.0.4"
      , "dnode" : "1.0.0"
      , "ejs": "0.8.3"
      , "express": "2.5.9"
      , "jquery" : "1.7.2"
      , "mocha": "1.0.1"
      , "mongodb": "1.1.7"
      , "should": "0.6.1"
      , "socket.io": "0.9.10"
```

```
    , "underscore": "1.3.3"
  }
}
```

Note that we specify both the Node.js version[6] and the npm version.[7] Since Heroku provides the platform, these versions are restricted to ones it officially supports.

Using the toolbelt, we can create the application with:

```
heroku create
```

It should come up with http://mysterious-brook-2122.herokuapp.com or similar.

So far so good, but now we have a problem. What do we do about the database? While Heroku does provide Node.js hosting, MongoDB is unsupported.[8] Remember the MongoLab account we created in the very first chapter? It is now time to come full circle. While knowing how to install MongoDB from scratch is a critical part of your Node.js journey, we'll now revisit a hosted deployment solution in order to provide compatibility with Heroku. So far, we've been connecting to the database locally with no need for credentials. We have to modify our database code to handle authentication. Modify **db.js** as follows:

chapter07/lib/db.js *(excerpt)*

```
open: function(callback) {
  db.open(function(err, data) {
    if (process.env.MONGO_NODE_DRIVER_USER) {
      data.authenticate(process.env.MONGO_NODE_DRIVER_USER
      , process.env.MONGO_NODE_DRIVER_PASS
      , function(err2, authData) {
        if(authData) { callback(); }
        else {
          console.log(err2);
          return;
        }
      });
    }
```

---

[6] http://heroku-buildpack-nodejs.s3.amazonaws.com/manifest.nodejs
[7] http://heroku-buildpack-nodejs.s3.amazonaws.com/manifest.npm
[8] There is an add-on available, but this requires registration with a credit card.

```
    else { callback(); }
  });
},
```

Heroku supports the use of environment variables, and here we look for the username and password in such variables. Depending on the version of Heroku you use, it may be necessary to specify the application name as well. If you receive an error message typing the following parameters into your console, try including the application name (the part in square brackets). Replace the *emphasized* parts with the parameters for your particular database:

```
heroku config:add MONGO_NODE_DRIVER_HOST=
➥XYZ.mongolab.com [--app mysterious-brook-2122]
heroku config:add MONGO_NODE_DRIVER_PORT=
➥12345 [--app mysterious-brook-2122]
heroku config:add MONGO_NODE_DRIVER_USER=
➥YOURUSER [--app mysterious-brook-2122]
heroku config:add MONGO_NODE_DRIVER_PASS=
➥YOURPASS [--app mysterious-brook-2122]
```

The parameters can be viewed and configured from your MongoLab account page.

Using a Remote Database Locally

With the modified database code, it is possible to run the database remotely if you do not wish to run a local copy of MongoDB. All you have to do is set the relevant environment variables. In Ubuntu, the command is as follows:

```
export MONGO_NODE_DRIVER_HOST=...
export MONGO_NODE_DRIVER_PORT=...
export MONGO_NODE_DRIVER_USER=...
export MONGO_NODE_DRIVER_PASS=...
```

After each line has been added, you should see a message on the console such as:

```
Adding config vars and restarting app... done, v5
```

We also use an environment variable to specify the port in **nockmarket.js** as follows:

```
                                    chapter07/nockmarket.js (excerpt)
db.open(function() {
  nocklib.createSocket(app);
  var port = process.env.PORT || 3000;
  app.listen(port);
  for (var i = 0; i < stocks.length; i++) {
    submitRandomOrder(i);
  }
});
```

This is necessary because Heroku prohibits applications from running on arbitrary ports. Instead, transient ports are used each time the application starts. `process.env.PORT` is actually set by Heroku, not our own application. This is all transparent to end users, who connect to our application the same way that they would connect to any other website.

One other small change is to parse the port as a number in **db.js**:

```
                                       chapter07/lib/db.js (excerpt)
, host = envHost != null ? envHost: 'localhost'
, port = envPort != null
  ? parseInt(envPort, 10) : Connection.DEFAULT_PORT;
```

Without this modification, the environment variable is interpreted as a string.

 Database Names

> On MongoLab, when creating a database you have the option of specifying a name. In the code, it is assumed that the database name is `'nockmarket'`, so I recommend you have or create a database with this name. Otherwise, it will be necessary to update **db.js** by replacing `'nockmarket'` with your actual database name in the following line:
>
> ```
>                                        chapter07/lib/db.js (excerpt)
> var db = new Db('nockmarket'
> ```

Now that we're deploying to a web server, we must modify the Socket.IO client code to connect to the actual web server. Modify **public/js/chat.js**:

chapter07/public/js/chat.js *(excerpt)*

```
var socket = io.connect(window.location.hostname);
```

Lastly, Heroku currently has no support for the WebSocket protocol. As discussed, one of the drawbacks of using PaaS is the need to conform to the rules and regulations that they apply. Modify **nocklib.js** to specify the transport mechanism:

chapter07/lib/nocklib.js *(excerpt)*

```
io.configure(function (){
  io.set("transports", ["xhr-polling"]);
  io.set("polling duration", 10);
  io.set('authorization', function (handshakeData, callback) {
```

Then we deploy the following to Heroku:

```
git add .
git commit -a -m "Ready for production"
git push heroku master
```

push is a git command that will transmit your local repository to a remote location. In this instance, we are pushing our local repository out to Heroku, at which point it will be automatically deployed. In fact, Heroku is open-source, so you're free to poke around the source code yourself to see how its deployment scripts run.[9]

 Idle Time

Behind the scenes, Heroku runs on EC2 infrastructure. This is not a cheap option, and so free accounts are "spun down" after a period of inactivity. The first user who connects after the idle period may need to wait a little longer while your application spins up. In practice, it's a minor issue, since the free accounts are geared more toward prototypes and testing rather than full-blown production systems. Paid accounts are not limited by this restriction.

If you receive an error message such as the following:

```
'heroku' does not appear to be a git repository
```

---

[9] https://github.com/heroku/heroku

... you can add the remote repository with this command:

```
git remote add heroku git@heroku.com: mysterious-brook-2122.git
```

Replace *mysterious-brook-2122* with your application name as assigned by Heroku.

You should now have a live system deployed on the Internet! Before we close the final curtain, let's add a personal touch. At the moment, the address is unfriendly. Having a personalized address is as simple as:

```
heroku rename YOURNAME
```

Your website's new address should appear in the console. Email your friends and family to let them see the wonderful piece of software that you've built. Perhaps they'll be inspired to implement that startup idea they've always dreamed of doing!

Summary

Congratulations, you've finally done it! In this chapter, we've learned the following:

- different options for hosting and some of the pros and cons for each
- using environment variables to control production settings
- how to handle 404 errors
- remote database access using the Node.js native MongoDB driver
- deploying to Heroku and the changes required for a production environment

Further Resources

Itching to learn more about Node.js? Here's a list of some great resources:

- Node.js API documentation: http://nodejs.org/api/
- MongoDB documentation: http://www.mongodb.org/display/DOCS/Home
- Backbone references: https://github.com/documentcloud/backbone/wiki/ Tutorials%2C-blog-posts-and-example-sites
- Socket.IO wiki: https://github.com/learnboost/socket.io/wiki
- DailyJS: A JavaScript blog: http://dailyjs.com/
- Scoop.it! Node.js resources: http://www.scoop.it/t/nodejs-code

Index

Hey ...

Thanks for buying this book. We really appreciate your support!

We'd like to think that you're now a "Friend of SitePoint," and so would like to invite you to our special "Friends of SitePoint" page.

Here you can SAVE up to 43% on a range of other super-cool SitePoint products.

Congratulations on Finishing the Book

Think of yourself as a bit of a natural with Node?

Time to test yourself with our online quiz. With questions based on the content in the book, only natural Node warriors can achieve a perfect score.

Take the Quiz Here:

http://quizpoint.com/#categories/NODE.JS.